THE C PUZZLE BOOK

Alan R. Feuer

Bell Laboratories
Murray Hill, New Jersey

PRENTICE-HALL, INC.,
Englewood Cliffs, NJ 07632

Library of Congress Cataloging in Publication Data

Feuer, Alan.
    The C puzzle book.

    (Prentice-Hall software series)
    Includes index.
    1. C (Computer program language)   2. UNIX (Computer
system)   I. Title.   II. Series.
QA76.73.C15F48   001.64′24   82-5302
ISBN 0-13-109934-5   AACR2
ISBN 0-13-109926-4 (pbk.)

Editorial/production supervision: Nancy Milnamow
Cover design: Ray Lundgren
Manufacturing buyer: Gordon Osbourne

Printed in the United States of America

10 9 8 7 6 5 4 3 2

ISBN 0-13-109934-5
ISBN 0-13-109926-4 {pbk.}

Prentice-Hall International, Inc., *London*
Prentice-Hall of Australia Pty. Limited, *Sydney*
Prentice-Hall of Canada, Ltd., *Toronto*
Prentice-Hall of India Private Limited, *New Delhi*
Prentice-Hall of Japan, Inc., *Tokyo*
Prentice-Hall of Southeast Asia Pte. Ltd., *Singapore*
Whitehall Books Limited, *Wellington, New Zealand*

THE C PUZZLE BOOK

PRENTICE-HALL SOFTWARE SERIES

Brian W. Kernighan, advisor

CONTENTS

SOLUTIONS

APPENDICES

PREFACE

C is not a large language. Measured by the weight of its reference manual, C could even be classified as small. The small size reflects a lack of confining rules rather than a lack of power. Users of C learn early to appreciate the elegance of expression afforded by its clear design.

Such elegance might seem needlessly arcane for new C programmers. The lack of restrictions means that C programs can be and are written with full-bodied expressions that may appear as printing errors to the novice. The cohesiveness of C often admits clear, but terse, ways to express common programming tasks.

The process of learning C, as for any programming language, may be modeled by three steps (no doubt repeated many times over). Step one is to understand the language syntax, at least to the point where the translator no longer complains of meaningless constructions. Step two is to know what meaning the translator will ascribe to properly formed constructions. And step three is to develop a programming style fitting for the language; it is the art of writing clear, concise, and correct programs.

The puzzles in this book are designed to help the reader through the second step. They will challenge the reader's mastery of the basic rules of C and lead the reader into seldom reached corners, beyond reasonable limits, and past a few open pits. (Yes, C, as all real languages, has its share of obscurities that are learned by experience.)

The puzzles should *not* be read as samples of good coding; indeed, some of the code is atrocious. But this is to be expected. Often the same qualities that make a program poor make a puzzle interesting:

- ambiguity of expression, requiring a rule book to interpret;

- complexity of structure, data and program structure not easily kept in one's head;

- obscurity of usage, using concepts in nonstandard ways.

C is still an evolving language. Depending upon the vintage of your local compiler, some of the features explored here may not be implemented and some of the implemented features may not be explored here. Fortunately, the evolution of C has proceeded uniformly, so it is very unlikely that your compiler will have a feature implemented in a different way than described here.

HOW TO USE THIS BOOK

The C Puzzle Book is a workbook intended to be used with a C language textbook such as *The C Programming Language* by Brian Kernighan and Dennis Ritchie (Prentice-Hall, 1978). This book is divided into sections with one major topic per section. Each section comprises C programs that explore different aspects of the section topic. The programs are sprinkled with print statements. The primary task is to discover what each program prints. All of the

vii

programs are independent of one another, though the later puzzles assume that you understand the properties of C illustrated in earlier puzzles.

The output for each program is given on the page following the text of the program. Each of the programs was run from the text under the UNIX† Operating System on Digital Equipment Corporation PDP 11/70 and VAX 11/780 computers. For the few cases where the output is different on the two machines, output is given from both.

The larger portion of the book is devoted to step-by-step derivations of the puzzle solutions. Many of the derivations are accompanied by tips and caveats for programming in C.

A typical scenario for using the puzzles might go like this:

- Read about a topic in the language textbook.
- For each program in the puzzle book section on the topic
  - Work the puzzles of the program.
  - Compare your answers to the program output.
  - Read the solution derivations.

ACKNOWLEDGEMENTS

The first C puzzles were developed for an introductory C programming course that I taught at Bell Laboratories. The encouraging response from students led me to hone the puzzles and embellish the solutions. A number of my friends and colleagues have given valuable comments and corrections to various drafts of this book. They are Al Boysen, Jr., Jeannette Feuer, Brian Kernighan, John Linderman, David Nowitz, Elaine Piskorik, Bill Roome, Keith Vollherbst, and Charles Wetherell. Finally, I am grateful for the fruitful environment and generous support provided me by Bell Laboratories.

Alan Feuer

---

† UNIX is a trademark of Bell Laboratories.

THE C PUZZLE BOOK

PUZZLES

Operators

C programs are built from statements, statements from expressions, and expressions from operators and operands. C is unusually rich in operators; see the operator summary of Appendix 2 if you need convincing. Because of this richness, the rules that determine how operators apply to operands play a central role in the understanding of expressions. The rules, known as precedence and associativity, are summarized in the precedence table of Appendix 1. Use the table to solve the problems in this section.

1

Operators 1: Basic Arithmetic Operators

What does the following program print?

```
main()
{
    int x;

    x = - 3 + 4 * 5 - 6; printf("%d\n",x);          (Operators 1.1)
    x = 3 + 4 % 5 - 6; printf("%d\n",x);            (Operators 1.2)
    x = - 3 * 4 % - 6 / 5; printf("%d\n",x);        (Operators 1.3)
    x = ( 7 + 6 ) % 5 / 2; printf("%d\n",x);        (Operators 1.4)
}
```

Operators 1: Basic Arithmetic Operators

OUTPUT:

1 1	*(Operators 1.1)*
1	*(Operators 1.2)*
0	*(Operators 1.3)*
1	*(Operators 1.4)*

Derivations begin on page 77.

Operators 2: Assignment Operators

What does the following program print?

```
#define PRINTX printf("%d\n",x)

main()
{
        int x=2, y, z;

        x *= 3 + 2; PRINTX;          (Operators 2.1)
        x *= y = z = 4; PRINTX;      (Operators 2.2)
        x = y == z; PRINTX;          (Operators 2.3)
        x == ( y = z ); PRINTX;      (Operators 2.4)
}
```

Operators 2: Assignment Operators

OUTPUT:

10	*(Operators 2.1)*
40	*(Operators 2.2)*
1	*(Operators 2.3)*
1	*(Operators 2.4)*

Derivations begin on page 80.

Operators 3: Logic and Increment Operators

What does the following program print?

```
#define PRINT(int) printf("%d\n",int)

main()
{
        int x, y, z;

        x = 2; y = 1; z = 0;
        x = x && y || z; PRINT(x);              (Operators 3.1)
        PRINT( x || ! y && z );                 (Operators 3.2)

        x = y = 1;
        z = x ++ - 1; PRINT(x); PRINT(z);       (Operators 3.3)
        z += - x ++ + ++ y; PRINT(x); PRINT(z); (Operators 3.4)
        z = x / ++ x; PRINT(z);                 (Operators 3.5)
}
```

Operators 3: Logic and Increment Operators

OUTPUT:

1	*(Operators 3.1)*
1	*(Operators 3.2)*
2	*(Operators 3.3)*
0	
3	*(Operators 3.4)*
0	
?	*(Operators 3.5)*

Derivations begin on page 83.

Operators 4: Bitwise Operators

What does the following program print?

```
#define PRINT(int) printf("int = %d\n",int)

main()
{
        int x, y, z;

        x = 03; y = 02; z = 01;
        PRINT( x | y & z );          (Operators 4.1)
        PRINT( x | y & ~ z );        (Operators 4.2)
        PRINT( x ^ y & ~ z );        (Operators 4.3)
        PRINT( x & y && z );         (Operators 4.4)

        x = 1; y = -1;
        PRINT( ! x | x );            (Operators 4.5)
        PRINT( ~ x | x );            (Operators 4.6)
        PRINT( x ^ x );              (Operators 4.7)
        x <<= 3; PRINT(x);           (Operators 4.8)
        y <<= 3; PRINT(y);           (Operators 4.9)
        y >>= 3; PRINT(y);           (Operators 4.10)
}
```

Operators 4: Bitwise Operators

OUTPUT:

x ¦ y & z = 3	*(Operators 4.1)*
x ¦ y & ~ z = 3	*(Operators 4.2)*
x ^ y & ~ z = 1	*(Operators 4.3)*
x & y && z = 1	*(Operators 4.4)*
! x ¦ x = 1	*(Operators 4.5)*
~ x ¦ x = -1	*(Operators 4.6)*
x ^ x = 0	*(Operators 4.7)*
x = 8	*(Operators 4.8)*
y = -8	*(Operators 4.9)*
y = ?	*(Operators 4.10)*

Derivations begin on page 86.

Operators 5: Relational and Conditional Operators

What does the following program print?

```
#define PRINT(int) printf("int = %d\n",int)

main()
{
        int x=1, y=1, z=1;

        x += y += z;
        PRINT( x < y ? y : x );                    (Operators 5.1)


        PRINT( x < y ? x ++ : y ++ );
        PRINT(x); PRINT(y);                        (Operators 5.2)


        PRINT( z += x < y ? x ++ : y ++ );
        PRINT(y); PRINT(z);                        (Operators 5.3)


        x=3; y=z=4;
        PRINT( (z >= y >= x) ? 1 : 0);             (Operators 5.4)
        PRINT( z >= y && y >= x );                 (Operators 5.5)
}
```

Operators 5: Relational and Conditional Operators

OUTPUT:

```
x < y ? y : x   = 3                    (Operators 5.1)
x < y ? x ++ : y ++   = 2              (Operators 5.2)
x = 3
y = 3
z += x < y ? x ++ : y ++   = 4         (Operators 5.3)
y = 4
z = 4
(z >= y >= x) ? 1 : 0 = 0              (Operators 5.4)
z >= y && y >= x   = 1                 (Operators 5.5)
```

Derivations begin on page 91.

Operators 6: Operator Precedence and Evaluation

What does the following program print?

```
#define PRINT3(x,y,z) printf("x=%d\ty=%d\tz=%d\n",x,y,z)

main()
{
    int x, y, z;

    x = y = z = 1;
    ++x || ++y && ++z; PRINT3(x,y,z);        (Operators 6.1)


    x = y = z = 1;
    ++x && ++y || ++z; PRINT3(x,y,z);        (Operators 6.2)


    x = y = z = 1;
    ++x && ++y && ++z; PRINT3(x,y,z);        (Operators 6.3)


    x = y = z = -1;
    ++x && ++y || ++z; PRINT3(x,y,z);        (Operators 6.4)


    x = y = z = -1;
    ++x || ++y && ++z; PRINT3(x,y,z);        (Operators 6.5)


    x = y = z = -1;
    ++x && ++y && ++z; PRINT3(x,y,z);        (Operators 6.6)
}
```

Operators 6: Operator Precedence and Evaluation

OUTPUT:

x = 2	y = 1	z = 1	*(Operators 6.1)*
x = 2	y = 2	z = 1	*(Operators 6.2)*
x = 2	y = 2	z = 2	*(Operators 6.3)*
x = 0	y = − 1	z = 0	*(Operators 6.4)*
x = 0	y = 0	z = − 1	*(Operators 6.5)*
x = 0	y = − 1	z = − 1	*(Operators 6.6)*

Derivations begin on page 94.

Basic Types

C has a comparatively small set of primitive types. The types may blindly be mixed in expressions, the results governed by a simple hierarchy of conversions. This hierarchy is illustrated in Appendix 4.

For some of the puzzles in this section you will need to know the corresponding integer value of some characters. The tables in Appendix 3 show the values for the characters in the ASCII set. A few of the puzzles yield a different result on the VAX than on the PDP 11. For those puzzles, output from both machines is given.

15

Basic Types 1: Character, String, and Integer Types

What does the following program print?

```
#include <stdio.h>

#define PRINT(format,x) printf("x = %format\n",x)

int  integer = 5;
char character = '5';
char *string = "5";

main()
{
     PRINT(d,string); PRINT(d,character); PRINT(d,integer);
     PRINT(s,string); PRINT(c,character); PRINT(c,integer=53);
     PRINT(d,( '5'>5 ));                        (Basic Types 1.1)

     {
         int sx = -8;
         unsigned ux = -8;

         PRINT(o,sx); PRINT(o,ux);
         PRINT(o, sx>>3 ); PRINT(o, ux>>3 );
         PRINT(d, sx>>3 ); PRINT(d, ux>>3 );    (Basic Types 1.2)
     }
}
```

Basic Types 1: Character, String, and Integer Types

OUTPUT:

```
string = an address   232206          (Basic Types 1.1)
character = 53   -
integer = 5   ✓
string = 5   -
character = 5   -
integer=53 = 5   ✓
( '5'>5 ) = 1   ✓
sx = 177770    377777777 ∅   (Basic Types 1.2-PDP 11)
ux = 177770    3777 777777 ∅
 sx>>3  = 177777 or 017777      37777777777
 ux>>3  = 17777                  37777777777
 sx>>3  = -1 or 8191
 ux>>3  = 8191


sx = 37777777770                 (Basic Types 1.2-VAX)
ux = 37777777770
 sx>>3  = 37777777777 or 03777777777
 ux>>3  = 3777777777
 sx>>3  = -1 or 536870911
 ux>>3  = 536870911
```

32 bit

-1

536870911

Derivations begin on page 97.

Basic Types 2: Integer and Floating Point Casts

What does the following program print?

```
#include <stdio.h>

#define PR(x)  printf("x = %.8g\t",(double)x)
#define NL putchar('\n')
#define PRINT4(x1,x2,x3,x4)  PR(x1); PR(x2); PR(x3); PR(x4); NL

main()
{
    double d;
    float f;
    long l;
    int i;

    i = l = f = d = 100/3; PRINT4(i,l,f,d);          (Basic Types 2.1)
    d = f = l = i = 100/3; PRINT4(i,l,f,d);          (Basic Types 2.2)
    i = l = f = d = 100/3.; PRINT4(i,l,f,d);         (Basic Types 2.3)
    d = f = l = i = (double)100/3;
    PRINT4(i,l,f,d);                                 (Basic Types 2.4)


    i = l = f = d = (double)(100000/3);
    PRINT4(i,l,f,d);                                 (Basic Types 2.5)

    d = f = l = i = 100000/3; PRINT4(i,l,f,d);       (Basic Types 2.6)
}
```

Basic Types 2: Integer and Floating Point Casts

OUTPUT:

```
i = 33   l = 33   f = 33   d = 33                        (Basic Types 2.1)
i = 33   l = 33   f = 33   d = 33                        (Basic Types 2.2)
i = 33   l = 33   f = 33.333332   d = 33.333333          (Basic Types 2.3)
i = 33   l = 33   f = 33   d = 33                        (Basic Types 2.4)
i = overflow   l = 33333   f = 33333   d = 33333     (Basic Types 2.5-PDP 11)
i = overflow   l = -32203   f = -32203   d = -32203  (Basic Types 2.6-PDP 11)
```

3.33333e+04   ✓   ✓   ✓

```
i = 33333   l = 33333   f = 33333   d = 33333        (Basic Types 2.5-VAX)
i = 33333   l = 33333   f = 33333   d = 33333        (Basic Types 2.6-VAX)
```

3.3333e+04

Derivations begin on page 99.

Basic Types 3: More Casts

What does the following program print?

```c
#include <stdio.h>

#define PR(x)  printf("x = %g\t",(double)(x))
#define NL putchar('\n')
#define PRINT1(x1)  PR(x1); NL
#define PRINT2(x1,x2)  PR(x1); PRINT1(x2)

main()
{
    double d=3.2, x;
    int i=2, y;

    x = (y=d/i)*2; PRINT2(x,y);                      (Basic Types 3.1)
    y = (x=d/i)*2; PRINT2(x,y);                      (Basic Types 3.2)

    y = d * (x=2.5/d); PRINT1(y);                    (Basic Types 3.3)
    x = d * (y = ((int)2.9+1.1)/d); PRINT2(x,y);     (Basic Types 3.4)
}
```

Basic Types 3: More Casts

OUTPUT:

x = 2	y = 1	*(Basic Types 3.1)*
x = 1.6	y = 3	*(Basic Types 3.2)*
y = 2		*(Basic Types 3.3)*
x = 0	y = 0	*(Basic Types 3.4)*

Derivations begin on page 103.

Included Files

Each of the remaining programs in this book begins with the preprocessor statement

```
#include "defs.h"
```

When the programs are compiled, the preprocessor replaces this line with the contents of the file defs.h, making the definitions in defs.h available for use. Here is a listing of defs.h:

```
#include <stdio.h>

#define PR(format,value) printf("value = %format\t",(value))
#define NL putchar('\n')

#define PRINT1(f,x1)  PR(f,x1), NL
#define PRINT2(f,x1,x2)  PR(f,x1), PRINT1(f,x2)
#define PRINT3(f,x1,x2,x3)  PR(f,x1), PRINT2(f,x2,x3)
#define PRINT4(f,x1,x2,x3,x4)  PR(f,x1), PRINT3(f,x2,x3,x4)
```

defs.h begins with an include statement of its own, calling for the insertion of the file stdio.h, as required by the standard C library. The rest of defs.h comprises macros for printing. As an example, to print 5 as a decimal number, the PRINT1 macro could be called by the expression

```
PRINT1(d,5)
```

which expands to

```
PR(d,5), NL
```

which further expands to

```
printf("5 = %d\t",(5)), putchar('\n').
```

The PRINT macros point out a feature of the preprocessor that often causes confusion. A macro name that appears inside a string (i.e., enclosed within double quotes) will not be expanded. However, argument names within the body of a macro will be replaced wherever they are found, even inside strings. Notice that the macro PR takes advantage of the latter property. See the Preprocessor Section, beginning on page 69, for a more detailed description of macro substitution.

Control Flow

1. `if` Statement
2. `while` and `for` Statements
3. Statement Nesting
4. `switch`, `break`, and `continue` Statements

C, as most programming languages, has control constructs for conditional selection and looping. To work the puzzles in this section, you will need to know how to determine the extent of each construct. In a well-formatted program, extent is indicated by indentation. Reading a poorly-formatted program is difficult and error prone; the following puzzles should convince you.

Control Flow 1: if Statement

What does the following program print?

```
#include "defs.h"

main()
{
    int x, y=1, z;

    if( y!=0 ) x=5;
    PRINT1(d,x);                    (Control Flow 1.1)

    if( y==0 ) x=3;
    else x=5;
    PRINT1(d,x);                    (Control Flow 1.2)

    x=1;
    if( y<0 ) if( y>0 ) x=3;
    else x=5;
    PRINT1(d,x);                    (Control Flow 1.3)

    if( z=y<0 ) x=3;
    else if( y==0 ) x=5;
    else x=7;
    PRINT2(d,x,z);                  (Control Flow 1.4)

    if( z=(y==0) ) x=5; x=3;
    PRINT2(d,x,z);                  (Control Flow 1.5)

    if( x=z=y ); x=3;
    PRINT2(d,x,z);                  (Control Flow 1.6)
}
```

Control Flow 1: if Statement

OUTPUT:

x = 5		*(Control Flow 1.1)*
x = 5		*(Control Flow 1.2)*
x = 1		*(Control Flow 1.3)*
x = 7	z = 0	*(Control Flow 1.4)*
x = 3	z = 0	*(Control Flow 1.5)*
x = 3	z = 1	*(Control Flow 1.6)*

Derivations begin on page 105.

Control Flow 2: while and for Statements

What does the following program print?

```
#include "defs.h"

main()
{
    int x, y, z;

    x=y=0;
    while( y<10 ) ++y; x += y;
    PRINT2(d,x,y);                        (Control Flow 2.1)


    x=y=0;
    while( y<10 ) x += ++y;
    PRINT2(d,x,y);                        (Control Flow 2.2)


    y=1;
    while( y<10 ) {
        x = y++; z = ++y;
    }
    PRINT3(d,x,y,z);                      (Control Flow 2.3)



    for( y=1; y<10; y++ ) x=y;
    PRINT2(d,x,y);                        (Control Flow 2.4)


    for( y=1; (x=y)<10; y++ ) ;
    PRINT2(d,x,y);                        (Control Flow 2.5)


    for( x=0,y=1000; y>1; x++,y/=10 )
        PRINT2(d,x,y);                    (Control Flow 2.6)

}
```

Control Flow 2: while and for Statements

OUTPUT:

x = 10 y = 10		*(Control Flow 2.1)*
x = 55 y = 10		*(Control Flow 2.2)*
x = 9 y = 11 z = 11		*(Control Flow 2.3)*
x = 9 y = 10		*(Control Flow 2.4)*
x = 10 y = 10		*(Control Flow 2.5)*
x = 0 y = 1000		*(Control Flow 2.6)*
x = 1 y = 100		
x = 2 y = 10		

Derivations begin on page 108.

Control Flow 3: Statement Nesting

What does the following program print?

```
#include "defs.h"

#define ENUF 3
#define EOS '\0'
#define NEXT(i) input[i++]
#define FALSE 0
#define TRUE 1

char input[]="PI=3.14159, approximately";

main()
{
    char c;
    int done, high, i, in, low;

    i=low=in=high=0;
    while( c=NEXT(i) != EOS )
        if( c<'0' ) low++;
        else if( c>'9' ) high++;
        else in++;
    PRINT3(d,low,in,high);                      (Control Flow 3.1)

    i=low=in=high=0; done=FALSE;
    while( (c=NEXT(i))!=EOS && !done )
        if( c<'0' ) low++;
        else if( c>'9' ) high++;
        else in++;
        if( low>=ENUF || high>=ENUF || in>=ENUF )
            done = TRUE;
    PRINT3(d,low,in,high);                      (Control Flow 3.2)

    i=low=in=high=0; done=FALSE;
    while( (c=NEXT(i))!=EOS && !done )
        if( c<'0' ) done = (++low==ENUF);
        else if( c>'9' ) done = (++high==ENUF);
        else done = (++in==ENUF);
    PRINT3(d,low,in,high);                      (Control Flow 3.3)
}
```

Control Flow 3: Statement Nesting

OUTPUT:

```
low = 25    in = 0    high = 0     (Control Flow 3.1)
low = 3     in = 6    high = 16    (Control Flow 3.2)
low = 0     in = 0    high = 3     (Control Flow 3.3)
```

Derivations begin on page 112.

Control Flow 4: `switch`, `break`, and `continue` Statements

What does the following program print?

```
#include "defs.h"

char input[] = "SSSWILTECH1\1\11W\1WALLMP1";

main()
{
    int i, c;

    for( i=2; (c=input[i])!='\0'; i++) {
        switch(c) {
        case 'a': putchar('i'); continue;
        case '1': break;
        case 1: while( (c=input[++i])!='\1' && c!='\0' ) ;
        case 9: putchar('S');
        case 'E': case 'L': continue;
        default: putchar(c); continue;
        }
        putchar(' ');
    }
    putchar('\n');                          (Control Flow 4.1)
}
```

Control Flow 4: switch, break, and continue Statements

OUTPUT:

SWITCH SWAMP   *(Control Flow 4.1)*

Derivation begins on page 114.

Programming Style

1. Choose the Right Condition
2. Choose the Right Construct

Much has been written about programming style, about which constructs to avoid and which to imitate. A cursory conclusion from the seemingly diverse advice is that good style is largely a matter of personal taste. A more reasoned conclusion is that good style in programming, as elsewhere, is a matter of good judgement. And while there are many good style guidelines, there are few always appropriate, always applicable style rules.

With this in mind, the following puzzles illustrate a few common style blunders. The solutions given are not so much answers, as in other sections, but rather alternatives. If there is an overall key to good style, it is a recognition of the final two steps in writing a readable program:

- Establish a clear statement of the idea to be coded.

- Develop the structure of the code from the structure of the idea statement.

Programming Style 1: Choose the Right Condition

Improve the following program fragments through reorganization.

```
while(A) {
    if(B) continue;
    C;
}
```
(Programming Style 1.1)

```
do {
    if(!A) continue;
    else B;
    C;
} while(A);
```
(Programming Style 1.2)

```
if(A)
    if(B)
        if(C) D;
        else;
    else;
else
    if(B)
        if(C) E;
        else F;
    else;
```
(Programming Style 1.3)

```
while( (c=getchar())!='\n' ) {
    if( c==' ' ) continue;
    if( c=='\t' ) continue;
    if( c<'0' ) return(OTHER);
    if( c<='9' ) return(DIGIT);
    if( c<'a' ) return(OTHER);
    if( c<='z' ) return(ALPHA);
    return(OTHER);
} return(EOL);
```
(Programming Style 1.4)

Derivations begin on page 117.

Programming Style 2: Choose the Right Construct

Improve the following program fragments through reorganization.

```
done=i=0;
while( i<MAXI && !done ) {
     if( (x/=2)>1 ) { i++; continue; }
     done++;
}
```
(Programming Style 2.1)

```
{
     if(A) { B; return; }
     if(C) { D; return; }
     if(E) { F; return; }
     G; return;
}
```
(Programming Style 2.2)

```
plusflg=zeroflg=negflg=0;
if( a>0 ) ++plusflg;
if( a==0 ) ++zeroflg;
else if( !plusflg ) ++negflg;
```
(Programming Style 2.3)

```
i=0;
while((c=getchar())!=EOF){
if(c!='\n'&&c!='\t'){s[i++]=c;continue;}
if(c=='\n')break;
if(c=='\t')c=' ';
s[i++]=c;}
```
(Programming Style 2.4)

```
if( x!=0 )
     if( j>k ) y=j/x;
     else y=k/x;
else
     if( j>k ) y=j/NEARZERO;
     else y=k/NEARZERO;
```
(Programming Style 2.5)

Derivations begin on page 119.

Storage Classes

Each variable in C possesses two fundamental properties, type and storage class. Type has been covered in an earlier section.

Storage class determines the scope and lifetime for a variable, scope being that part of a program in which a variable is known and lifetime being that portion of an execution during which a variable has a value. The boundaries of scope and lifetime are blocks, functions, and files.

Storage Classes 1: Blocks

What does the following program print?

```
#include "defs.h"

int i=0;

main()
{
    auto int i=1;
    PRINT1(d,i);
    {
        int i=2;
        PRINT1(d,i);
        {
            i += 1;
            PRINT1(d,i);
        }
        PRINT1(d,i);
    }
    PRINT1(d,i);                      (Storage Classes 1.1)
}
```

Storage Classes 1: Blocks

OUTPUT:

```
i = 1          (Storage Classes 1.1)
i = 2
i = 3
i = 3
i = 1
```

Derivations begin on page 123.

Storage Classes 2: Functions

What does the following program print?

```c
#include "defs.h"

#define LOW 0
#define HIGH 5
#define CHANGE 2

int i=LOW;

main()
{
    auto int i=HIGH;
    reset( i/2 ); PRINT1(d,i);
    reset( i=i/2 ); PRINT1(d,i);
    i = reset( i/2 ); PRINT1(d,i);

    workover(i); PRINT1(d,i);          (Storage Classes 2.1)
}

workover(i)
int i;
{
    i = (i%i) * ((i*i)/(2*i) + 4);
    PRINT1(d,i);
    return(i);
}

int reset(i)
int i;
{
    i = i<=CHANGE ? HIGH : LOW;
    return(i);
}
```

Storage Classes 2: Functions

OUTPUT:

```
i = 5        (Storage Classes 2.1)
i = 2
i = 5
i = 0
i = 5
```

Derivations begin on page 124.

Storage Classes 3: More Functions

What does the following program print?

```
#include "defs.h"
int i=1;

main()
{
     auto int i, j;
     i = reset();
     for( j=1; j<=3; j++ ) {
          PRINT2(d,i,j);
          PRINT1(d,next(i));
          PRINT1(d,last(i));
          PRINT1(d,new(i+j));          (Storage Classes 3.1)
     }
}

int reset()
{
     return(i);
}

int next(j)
int j;
{
     return( j=i++ );
}

int last(j)
int j;
{
     static int i=10;
     return( j=i-- );
}

int new(i)
int i;
{
     auto int j=10;
     return( i=j+=i );
}
```

Storage Classes 3: More Functions

OUTPUT:

```
i = 1     j = 1     (Storage Classes 3.1)
next(i) = 1
last(i) = 10
new(i+j) = 12
i = 1     j = 2
next(i) = 2
last(i) = 9
new(i+j) = 13
i = 1     j = 3
next(i) = 3
last(i) = 8
new(i+j) = 14
```

Derivations begin on page 125

Storage Classes 4: Files

nt?

```
            j++ ) {
          j);
        ext(i));
        ast(i));
        ew(i+j));
```

(Storage Classes 4.1)

In yet another file

```
extern int i;

reset()
{
    return(i);
}
```

```
{
        return( i+=1 );
}

int last()
{
        return( i-=1 );
}

int new(i)
int i;
{
        static int j=5;
        return( i=j+=i );
}
```

Storage Classes 4: Files

OUTPUT:

```
i = 1      j = 1      (Storage Classes 4.1)
next(i) = 11
last(i) = 10
new(i+j) = 7
i = 1      j = 2
next(i) = 11
last(i) = 10
new(i+j) = 10
i = 1      j = 3
next(i) = 11
last(i) = 10
new(i+j) = 14
```

Derivations begin on page 127.

Pointers and Arrays

Pointers have long been abused by programmers and thus maligned in style guides. Specifically, pointers are criticized since, by their nature, it is impossible to identify fully a pointer's referent without backing up to where the pointer was last defined; this adds complexity to a program and makes verification much more difficult.

The C language, rather than restricting the use of pointers, often makes them the natural choice for use. As the following puzzles will illustrate, pointers and arrays are very closely related. For any application using array indexing, a pointer version also exists. The warnings against the dangers of pointer misuse apply as strongly to C as to any language.

Pointers and Arrays 1: Simple Pointer and Array

What does the following program print?

```
#include "defs.h"

int a[]={0,1,2,3,4};

main()
{
    int i, *p;

    for( i=0; i<=4; i++ ) PR(d,a[i]);            (Pointers and Arrays 1.1)
    NL;
    for( p= &a[0]; p<=&a[4]; p++ )
        PR(d,*p);                                (Pointers and Arrays 1.2)
    NL; NL;

    for( p= &a[0],i=1; i<=5; i++ )
        PR(d,p[i]);                              (Pointers and Arrays 1.3)
    NL;
    for( p=a,i=0; p+i<=a+4; p++,i++ )
        PR(d,*(p+i));                            (Pointers and Arrays 1.4)
    NL; NL;

    for( p=a+4; p>=a; p-- ) PR(d,*p);            (Pointers and Arrays 1.5)
    NL;
    for( p=a+4,i=0; i<=4; i++ ) PR(d,p[-i]);     (Pointers and Arrays 1.6)
    NL;
    for( p=a+4; p>=a; p-- ) PR(d,a[p-a]);        (Pointers and Arrays 1.7)
    NL;
```

Pointers and Arrays 1: Simple Pointer and Array

OUTPUT:

a[i] = 0   a[i] = 1   a[i] = 2   a[i] = 3   a[i] = 4
(Pointers and Arrays 1.1)

*p = 0   *p = 1   *p = 2   *p = 3   *p = 4
(Pointers and Arrays 1.2)

p[i] = 1   p[i] = 2   p[i] = 3   p[i] = 4   p[i] = ?
(Pointers and Arrays 1.3)

*(p+i) = 0 *(p+i) = 2 *(p+i) = 4   *(Pointers and Arrays 1.4)*

*p = 4   *p = 3   *p = 2   *p = 1   *p = 0
(Pointers and Arrays 1.5)

p[-i] = 4   p[-i] = 3   p[-i] = 2   p[-i] = 1   p[-i] = 0
(Pointers and Arrays 1.6)

a[p-a] = 4 a[p-a] = 3 a[p-a] = 2 a[p-a] = 1 a[p-a] = 0
(Pointers and Arrays 1.7)

Derivations begin on page 129.

Pointers and Arrays 2: Array of Pointers

What does the following program print?

```
#include "defs.h"

int a[]={0,1,2,3,4};
int *p[]={a,a+1,a+2,a+3,a+4};
int **pp=p;                                    (Pointers and Arrays 2.1)

main()
{
    PRINT2(d,a,*a);
    PRINT3(d,p,*p,**p);
    PRINT3(d,pp,*pp,**pp);                     (Pointers and Arrays 2.2)
    NL;

    pp++; PRINT3(d,pp-p,*pp-a,**pp);
    *pp++; PRINT3(d,pp-p,*pp-a,**pp);
    *++pp; PRINT3(d,pp-p,*pp-a,**pp);
    ++*pp; PRINT3(d,pp-p,*pp-a,**pp);          (Pointers and Arrays 2.3)
    NL;

    pp=p;
    **pp++; PRINT3(d,pp-p,*pp-a,**pp);
    *++*pp; PRINT3(d,pp-p,*pp-a,**pp);
    ++**pp; PRINT3(d,pp-p,*pp-a,**pp);         (Pointers and Arrays 2.4)
}
```

Pointers and Arrays 2: Array of Pointers

OUTPUT:

a = address of a	*a = 0		*(Pointers and Arrays 2.2)*
p = address of p	*p = address of a	**p = 0	
pp = address of p	*pp = address of a	**pp = 0	

pp-p = 1	*pp-a = 1	**pp = 1	*(Pointers and Arrays 2.3)*
pp-p = 2	*pp-a = 2	**pp = 2	
pp-p = 3	*pp-a = 3	**pp = 3	
pp-p = 3	*pp-a = 4	**pp = 4	

pp-p = 1	*pp-a = 1	**pp = 1	*(Pointers and Arrays 2.4)*
pp-p = 1	*pp-a = 2	**pp = 2	
pp-p = 1	*pp-a = 2	**pp = 3	

Derivations begin on page 132.

Pointers and Arrays 3: Multidimensional Array

What does the following program print?

```
#include "defs.h"

int a[3][3] = {
     { 1, 2, 3 },
     { 4, 5, 6 },
     { 7, 8, 9 }
};
int *pa[3] = {
     a[0], a[1], a[2]
};
int *p = a[0];                              (Pointers and Arrays 3.1)

main()
{
     int i;

     for( i=0; i<3; i++ )
          PRINT3(d, a[i][2-i], *a[i], *(*(a+i)+i) );
     NL;                                    (Pointers and Arrays 3.2)

     for( i=0; i<3; i++ )
          PRINT2(d, *pa[i], p[i] );         (Pointers and Arrays 3.3)
}
```

Pointers and Arrays 3: Multidimensional Array

OUTPUT:

```
a[i][2-i] = 3    *a[i] = 1  *(*(a+i)+i)  = 1    (Pointers and Arrays 3.2)
a[i][2-i] = 5    *a[i] = 4  *(*(a+i)+i)  = 5
a[i][2-i] = 7    *a[i] = 7  *(*(a+i)+i)  = 9

*pa[i] = 1       p[i]  = 1                       (Pointers and Arrays 3.3)
*pa[i] = 4       p[i]  = 2
*pa[i] = 7       p[i]  = 3
```

Derivations begin on page 136.

Pointers and Arrays 4: Pointer Stew

What does the following program print?

```
#include "defs.h"

char *c[] = {
    "ENTER",
    "NEW",
    "POINT",
    "FIRST"
};
char **cp[] = { c+3, c+2, c+1, c };
char ***cpp = cp;                        (Pointers and Arrays 4.1)

main()
{
    printf("%s", **++cpp );
    printf("%s ", *--*++cpp+3 );
    printf("%s", *cpp[-2]+3 );
    printf("%s\n", cpp[-1][-1]+1 );      (Pointers and Arrays 4.2)
}
```

Pointers and Arrays 4: Pointer Stew

OUTPUT:

POINTER STEW   *(Pointers and Arrays 4.1)*

Derivation begins on page 138.

Structures

A structure, that is the C data type `struct`, is a fundamental building block for data structures. It provides a convenient way to package dissimilar but related data items.

Structures 1: Simple Structure, Nested Structure

What does the following program print?

```
#include "defs.h"

main()
{
    static struct S1 {
        char c[4], *s;
    } s1 = { "abc", "def" };

    static struct S2 {
        char *cp;
        struct S1 ss1;
    } s2 = { "ghi", { "jkl", "mno" } };        (Structures 1.1)

    PRINT2(c, s1.c[0], *s1.s);                 (Structures 1.2)
    PRINT2(s, s1.c, s1.s);                     (Structures 1.3)

    PRINT2(s, s2.cp, s2.ss1.s);                (Structures 1.4)
    PRINT2(s, ++s2.cp, ++s2.ss1.s);            (Structures 1.5)
}
```

Structures 1: Simple Structure, Nested Structure

OUTPUT:

s1.c[0] = a	*s1.s = d	*(Structures 1.2)*
s1.c = abc	s1.s = def	*(Structures 1.3)*
s2.cp = ghi	s2.ss1.s = mno	*(Structures 1.4)*
++s2.cp = hi	++s2.ss1.s = no	*(Structures 1.5)*

Derivations begin on page 141.

Structures 2: Array of Structures

What does the following program print?

```
#include "defs.h"

struct S1 {
    char *s;
    int i;
    struct S1 *s1p;
};

main()
{
    static struct S1 a[] = {
        { "abcd", 1, a+1 },
        { "efgh", 2, a+2 },
        { "ijkl", 3, a }
    };
    struct S1 *p = a;                          (Structures 2.1)
    int i;

    PRINT3(s, a[0].s, p->s, a[2].s1p->s);      (Structures 2.2)

    for( i=0; i<2; i++ ) {
        PR(d, --a[i].i);
        PR(c, ++a[i].s[3]);                    (Structures 2.3)
        NL;
    }

    PRINT3(s, ++(p->s), a[(++p)->i].s, a[--(p->s1p->i)].s);
                                               (Structures 2.4)
}
```

Structures 2: Array of Structures

OUTPUT:

```
a[0].s = abcd    p->s = abcd              a[2].s1p->s = abcd
                                                   (Structures 2.2)
--a[i].i = 0     ++a[i].s[3] = e                   (Structures 2.3)
--a[i].i = 1     ++a[i].s[3] = i
++(p->s) = bce   a[(++p)->i].s = efgi  a[--(p->s1p->i)].s = ijkl
                                                   (Structures 2.4)
```

Derivations begin on page 145.

Structures 3: Array of Pointers to Structures

What does the following program print?

```
#include "defs.h"
struct S1 {
    char *s;
    struct S1 *s1p;
};

main()
{
    static struct S1 a[] = {
        { "abcd", a+1 },
        { "efgh", a+2 },
        { "ijkl", a }
    };
    struct S1 *p[3];                                    (Structures 3.1)
    int i;

    for( i=0; i<3; i++ ) p[i] = a[i].s1p;
    PRINT3(s, p[0]->s, (*p)->s, (**p).s);               (Structures 3.2)

    swap(*p,a);
    PRINT3(s, p[0]->s, (*p)->s, (*p)->s1p->s);          (Structures 3.3)

    swap(p[0], p[0]->s1p);
    PRINT3(s, p[0]->s, (*++p[0]).s, ++(*++(*p)->s1p).s);
                                                        (Structures 3.4)
}

swap(p1,p2)
struct S1 *p1, *p2;
{
    char *temp;

    temp = p1->s;
    p1->s = p2->s;
    p2->s = temp;
}
```

Structures 3: Array of Pointers to Structures

OUTPUT:

```
p[0]->s = efgh    (*p)->s = efgh   (**p).s = efgh           (Structures 3.2)
p[0]->s = abcd    (*p)->s = abcd   (*p)->s1p->s = ijkl (Structures 3.3)
p[0]->s = ijkl    (*++p[0]).s = abcd     ++(*++(*p)->s1p).s = jkl
                                                          (Structures 3.4)
```

Derivations begin on page 152.

Preprocessor

Though in a strict sense the preprocessor is not part of the C language, few C programs would compile without it. Its two most important functions are macro substitution and file inclusion.

This section concentrates on macro substitution. When used judiciously, macros are a versatile tool that can enhance the readability and efficiency of a program. When used unwisely, macros, like other features in C, can lead to insidious bugs. To solve the puzzles in this section, follow the rules for expanding macros *very* carefully.

Preprocessor 1: The Preprocessor Doesn't Know C

What does the following program print?

```c
#include <stdio.h>
#define FUDGE(k)    k+3.14159
#define PR(a)  printf("a= %d\t",(int)(a))
#define PRINT(a)     PR(a); putchar('\n')
#define PRINT2(a,b) PR(a); PRINT(b)
#define PRINT3(a,b,c)    PR(a); PRINT2(b,c)
#define MAX(a,b)     (a<b ? b : a)

main()
{

    {
        int x=2;
        PRINT( x*FUDGE(2) );                    (Preprocessor 1.1)
    }


    {
        int cel;
        for( cel=0; cel<=100; cel+=50 )
            PRINT2( cel, 9./5*cel+32 );         (Preprocessor 1.2)
    }


    {
        int x=1, y=2;
        PRINT3( MAX(x++,y),x,y );
        PRINT3( MAX(x++,y),x,y );               (Preprocessor 1.3)
    }

}
```

Preprocessor 1: The Preprocessor Doesn't Know C

OUTPUT:

```
x*FUDGE(2)  = 7                                         (Preprocessor 1.1)
cel= 0      cel= 50    cel= 100   9./5*cel+32  = 302    (Preprocessor 1.2)
MAX(x++,y)= 2          x= 2       y = 2                 (Preprocessor 1.3)
MAX(x++,y)= 3          x= 4       y = 2
```

Derivations begin on page 158.

Preprocessor 2: Caution Pays

What does the following program print?

```
#include <stdio.h>
#define NEG(a)-a
#define weeks(mins)  (days(mins)/7)
#define days(mins)   (hours(mins)/24)
#define hours(mins)  (mins/60)
#define mins(secs)   (secs/60)
#define TAB(c,i,oi,t)     if(c=='\t')\
                             for(t=8-(i-oi-1)%8,oi=i; t; t--)\
                               putchar(' ')
#define PR(a)        printf("a= %d\t",(int)(a))
#define PRINT(a)     PR(a); putchar('\n')

main()
{
    {
        int x=1;
        PRINT( -NEG(x) );                          (Preprocessor 2.1)
    }

    {
        PRINT( weeks(10080) );
        PRINT( days(mins(86400)) );                (Preprocessor 2.2)
    }

    {
        static char input[] = "\twhich\tif?";
        char c;
        int i, oldi, temp;

        for( oldi= -1,i=0; (c=input[i])!='\0'; i++ )
            if( c<' ' ) TAB(c,i,oldi,temp);
            else putchar(c);
            putchar('\n');                         (Preprocessor 2.3)
    }
}
```

Preprocessor 2: Caution Pays

OUTPUT:

```
-NEG(x)= 0                              (Preprocessor 2.1)
weeks(10080) = 1                        (Preprocessor 2.2)
days(mins(86400)) = 1
eleven spaces                           (Preprocessor 2.3)
```

Derivations begin on page 161.

SOLUTIONS

Operators 1.1

`x = - 3 + 4 * 5 - 6`	Begin by reading the precedence table in Appendix 1 from high to low.
`x = (-3) + 4 * 5 - 6`	The highest level operator in the expression is the unary –. We'll use parentheses to indicate the order of binding operands to operators.
`x = (-3) + (4*5) - 6`	Next highest in the expression is *.
`x = ((-3)+(4*5)) - 6`	Both + and – are at the same precedence level. The order of binding thus depends on the associativity rule for that level. For + and –, associativity is left to right. First the + is bound.
`x = (((-3)+(4*5))-6)`	And then the –.
`(x=(((-3)+(4*5))-6))`	And finally, near the bottom of the precedence table, is =. Now that we have completely identified the operands for each operator, we can evaluate the expression.
`(x=((-3+(4*5))-6)`	For this expression, evaluation proceeds from the inside out.
`(x=((-3+20)-6)`	Replace each subexpression by its resulting value.
`(x=(17-6))`	
`(x=11)`	
`11, an integer`	The value of an assignment expression is the value of the right-hand side cast in the type of the left-hand side.

About printf. `Printf` is the formatted print routine that comes as part of the standard C library. The first argument to `printf` is a format string. It describes how any remaining arguments are to be printed. The character % begins a print specification for an argument. In our program, `%d` told `printf` to interpret and print the next argument as a decimal number. We will see other print specifications in later programs. `Printf` can also output literal characters. In our program, we "printed" a newline character by giving its name (\n) in the format string.

Operators 1.2

`x = 3 + 4 % 5 - 6`	This expression is very similar to the previous one.
`x = 3 + ( 4%5 ) - 6`	Following precedence
`x = ( 3+( 4%5 ) ) - 6`	and associativity
`x = ( ( 3+( 4%5 ) )-6 )`	leads to
`( x=( ( 3+( 4%5 ) )-6 ) )`	this. (The modulo, %, operator yields the remainder of dividing 4 by 5.)
`( x=( ( 3+4 )-6 )`	Again, evaluation is from the inside out.
`( x=( 7-6 ) )`	
`( x=1 )`	
`1`	

Operators 1.3

`x = - 3 * 4 % - 6 / 5`	This expression is a bit more complex than the last, but rigorous adherence to precedence and associativity will untangle it.
`x = (-3) * 4 % (-6) / 5`	
`x = ( (-3)*4) % (-6) / 5`	*, %, and / are all at the same precedence level, and they associate from left to right.
`x = ( ( (-3)*4)%(-6) ) / 5`	
`x = ( ( ( (-3)*4)%(-6) )/5 )`	
`( x=( ( ( (-3)*4)%(-6) )/5 ) )`	
`( x=( ( (-3*4)%-6)/5 ) )`	Evaluating from the inside out.
`( x=( ( -12%-6)/5 ) )`	
`( x=( 0/5 ) )`	
`( x=0 )`	
`0`	

Operators 1.4

`x = ( 7 + 6 ) % 5 / 2`	Of course we are not totally at the mercy of predefined precedence. Parentheses can always be used to effect or clarify a meaning.
`x = (7+6) % 5 / 2`	Subexpressions within parentheses bind first.
`x = ((7+6)%5) / 2`	Then, it is according to the precedence and associativity rules as before.
`x = (((7+6)%5)/2)`	
`(x=(((7+6)%5)/2))`	
`(x=((13%5)/2))`	Evaluating.
`(x=(3/2))`	
`(x=1)`	Integer arithmetic truncates any fractional part.
`1`	

About programming style. As mentioned in the Preface, the programs in this book are not models to be copied. They were designed to make you think about the mechanics of how C works. But the puzzles do contain messages about program style. If a construct always forces you to consult a reference to find out how some detail is handled, then the construct is either not well written or it should be accompanied by a comment that provides the missing details.

The message from this first set of puzzles is to use parentheses in complex expressions to help the reader associate operands with operators.

Operators 2.1

initially **x**=**2**

x ***= 3 + 2**   Again follow the precedence table.

x ***= (3+2)**   As we saw earlier, the assignment operators have lower precedence than the arithmetic operators. (***=** is an assignment operator.)

(x*=(3+2))

(x*=5)   Evaluating.

(x = x*5)   Expanding the assignment to its equivalent form.

(x=10)

10

About define. This program begins with the line

```
#define PRINTX printf( "%d\n",x )
```

Any line in a C program that begins with the character **#** is a statement to the C preprocessor. One job done by the preprocessor is the substitution of one string by another. The **define** statement in this program tells the preprocessor to replace all instances of the string PRINTX with the string **printf("%d\n",x)**.

Operators 2.2

initially **x** = 1 0

x *= y = z = 4

x *= y = (z = 4)   In this expression all the operators are assignments, hence associativity determines the order of binding. Assignment operators associate from right to left.

x *= (y=(z=4))

(x *= (y=(z=4)))

(x *= (y=4))   Evaluating.

(x *= 4)

4 0

Operators 2.3

initially y=4 , z=4

x = y == z

x = (y==z)   Often a source of confusion for programmers new to C is the distinction between = (assignment) and == (test for equality). From the precedence table it can be seen that == is bound before =.

(x=(y==z))

(x=(TRUE))

(x=1)   Relational and equality operators yield a result of TRUE, an integer 1, or FALSE, an integer 0.

1

Operators 2.4

initially **x**=1, **z**=4

x == (**y** = **z**)

(x==(y=z))   In this expression the assignment has been forced to have higher precedence than the test for equality through the use of parentheses.

(x==4)   Evaluating.

FALSE, or 0   The value of the expression is 0. Note however that the value of **x** has not changed (== does not change its operands), so PRINTX prints 1.

Operators 3.1

initially x=2, y=1, z=0

x = x && y ¦¦ z

x = (x&&y) ¦¦ z   Bind operands to operators according to precedence.

x = ((x&&y)¦¦z)

(x=((x&&y)¦¦z))

(x=((TRUE&&TRUE)¦¦z))   Logical operators are evaluated from left to right.
                                   An operand to a logical operator is FALSE if it is
                                   zero and TRUE if it is anything else.

(x=(TRUE¦¦z))   The logical AND, &&, yields TRUE only when both
                                   its operands are TRUE, otherwise FALSE.

(x=(TRUE¦¦whatever))   Once one argument to the OR, ¦¦, is known to be
                                   TRUE we know the result of the ¦¦ will be TRUE
                                   regardless of the other operand. Hence there is no
                                   need to evaluate the expression further.

(x=TRUE)

(x=1)

1

More about define. The define statement that begins this program is a little fancier than that in the previous program. Here, PRINT is the name of a *macro with arguments,* not just a simple string. The preprocessor performs two levels of substitution on macros with arguments: first the actual arguments are substituted for the formal arguments in the macro body, and then the resulting macro body is substituted for the macro call.

For example, in this program PRINT has one formal argument, int. PRINT(x) is a call of PRINT with the actual argument x. Thus, each occurrence of int in the macro body is first replaced by x, and then the resulting string, printf("%d\n",x), is substituted for the call, PRINT(x). Notice that the formal parameter int did not match the middle letters in printf. This is because the formal arguments of a macro are identifiers; int only matches the *identifier* int.

Operators 3.2

initially x=1, y=1, z=0

x ¦¦ ! y && z

x ¦¦ (!y) && z   Binding operands to operators.

x ¦¦ ((!y)&&z)

(x¦¦((!y)&&z))

(TRUE¦¦((!y)&&z))   Evaluating from left to right.

(TRUE¦¦whatever)

TRUE, or 1

Operators 3.3

initially x=1, y=1

z = x ++ - 1

z = (x++) - 1   Following precedence.

z = ((x++)-1)

(z=((x++)-1))

(z=(1-1)), and x=2   The ++ to the right of its operand is a post increment. This means that x is incremented after its value is used in the expression.

(z=0)

0

Operators 3.4

initially x=2 , y=1 , z=0

z += - x ++ + ++ y

z += - (x++) + (++y)

Unary operators associate from right to left, thus ++ binds before unary -. (Actually, the expression would not be legal if it were arranged so that the - bound first since ++ and -- expect a reference to a variable (an lvalue) as their operand. x is an lvalue, but -x is not.)

z += (-(x++)) + (++y)

z += ((-(x++))+(++y))

(z+=((-(x++))+(++y)))

(z+=((-2)+2)) , and x=3 , y=2   Evaluating from the inside out.

(z+=0)

(z = 0+0)

(z=0)

0

Operators 3.5

initially x=3 , z=0

z = x / ++ x

z = x / (++x)

z = (x/(++x))

(z=(x/(++x)))

You may be tempted at this point to begin evaluating this expression as before, from the inside out. First the value of x would be retrieved and incremented to be divided into the value of x. One question that might be asked is what value is retrieved from x for the numerator, 3 or 4? That is, is the value for the numerator retrieved before or after the increment is stored? The C language does not specify when such a side effect[1] actually occurs; that is left to the compiler writer. The message is to avoid writing expressions that depend upon knowing when a side effect will occur.

---

1. A side effect is any change to the state of a program that occurs as a byproduct of executing a statement. By far the most common side effects in C relate to storing intermediate values in variables, such as with the increment operator as above or with an embedded assignment operator.

Operators 4.1

initially **x**=03, **y**=02, **z**=01

x ¦ y & z

Integer constants preceded by 0 (zero) are octal values. Octal notation is particularly useful when working with the bitwise operators because it is easy to translate octal numbers to binary. In this problem, 01, 02, and 03 are equivalent to 1, 2, and 3, so using octal is merely a cue to the reader that the program will deal with the values of **x**, **y**, and **z** as bit strings.

(**x ¦ (y&z)**)

Following precedence.

(**x ¦ (02&01)**)

The innermost expression is evaluated first.

(**x ¦ 0**)

In binary, 01 = 1, 02 = 10, 03 = 11

```
      10
&   01
  ----
      00
```

(03¦0)

03

```
      00
¦   11
  ----
      11
```

Operators 4.2

initially **x=03**, **y=02**, **z=01**

x ¦ y & ~ z

(x ¦ (y & (~ z)))

(x ¦ (y & ~ 0 1))   ~ complements each of the bits of its operand.
                                                   Thus 0 . . . 0 1 becomes 1 . . . 1 0.

(x ¦ (0 2 & ~ 0 1))

(0 3 ¦ 0 2)   In binary,

```
        0...010
   &    1...110
   ----------
        0000010
```

3

```
        10
   ¦    11
   ----
        11
```

Operators 4.3

initially **x=03**, **y=02**, **z=01**

x ^ y & ~ z

(x ^ (y & (~ z)))   This is the same as the previous problem except
                                                   that the exclusive or, ^, has been substituted for
                                                   the inclusive or, ¦.

(x ^ (0 2 & ~ 0 1))

(0 3 ^ 0 2)

1   In binary,

```
        10
   ^    11
   ----
        01
```

Operators 4.4

```
initially x=03, y=02, z=01
x & y && z
((x&y)&&z)
((03&02)&&z)
(02&&z)
(TRUE&&z)
(TRUE&&01)
(TRUE&&TRUE)
TRUE, or 1
```
&& yields TRUE whenever both operands are
TRUE.

Operators 4.5

```
initially x=01
! x ¦ x
((!x)¦x)
((!TRUE)¦x)
(FALSE¦01)
(0¦01)
1
```

Operators 4.6

initially x = 0 1

~ x ¦ x

((~ x) ¦ x)

(~ 0 1 ¦ 0 1)

– 1   In binary,

```
    1...110
¦ 0...001
---------
    1...111,  or  – 1
```

(The answer is the same for all values of x. Actually, it is – 1 on a two's-complement machine, like the PDP-11. On a one's-complement machine 1 . . . 1 would be – 0. For the few cases in this book where it matters, two's-complement will be used.)

Operators 4.7

initially x = 0 1

x ^ x

(0 1 ^ 0 1)

0   In binary,

```
    0...01
^ 0...01
--------
    0...00
```

(The answer is the same for all values of x.)

Operators 4.8

initially x = 0 1

x < < = 3

x = 0 1 < < 3

x = 8   In binary,

```
            0 0 0 0 . . . 0 1
       < <                 3
       - - - - - - - - - -
                 0 . . . 0 1 0 0 0 ,  which is  8
```

Each place shifted to the left is an effective multiplication by 2.

Operators 4.9

initially y = - 0 1

y < < = 3

y = - 0 1 < < 3

y = - 8   In binary,

```
            1 1 1 1 . . . 1 1
       < <                 3
       - - - - - - - - - -
                 1 . . . 1 1 0 0 0 ,  or  - 8
```

Operators 4.10

initially y = - 0 8

y > > = 3

y = - 0 8 > > 3

It is tempting at this point to assume that y = - 1. Unfortunately this is not always the case, since the computer may not preserve the sign of a number when shifting. C does not guarantee that the shift will be arithmetically correct. In any case, there is a much clearer way to divide by 8, namely y = y / 8.

Operators 5.1

    initially x=3 , y=2 , z=1

    x < y ? y : x

    (x<y) ? (y) : (x)   The conditional operator, aside from taking three operands, is parsed like any other operator.

    ((x<y) ? (y) : (x))

    (FALSE? (y) : (x))   First the condition is evaluated. Then either the true part or the false part is evaluated, but not both.

    ((x))   In this problem the value of the condition is FALSE, thus the value of the conditional expression is the value of the false part.

    (3)

    3

Operators 5.2

    initially x=3 , y=2 , z=1

    x < y ? x ++ : y ++

    ((x<y) ? (x++) : (y++))

    (FALSE? (x++) : (y++))   First evaluate the condition.

    ((y++))   The condition is FALSE so the false part is evaluated.

    (2) , and y=3

    2   (And since x++ was not evaluated, x remains 3.)

Operators 5.3

```
initially x=3 , y=3 , z=1
z += x < y ? x ++ : y ++
( z+=( ( x<y ) ? ( x++ ) : ( y++ ) ) )
( z+=( FALSE? ( x++ ) : ( y++ ) ) )
( z+=( ( y++ ) )
```

The result of the conditional expression is the right-hand side of the assignment.

```
( z+=( 3 ) ) , and y=4
( z=z+3 )
( z=4 )
4
```

Operators 5.4

```
initially x=3 , y=4 , z=4
( z >= y >= x ) ? 1 : 0
( ( ( z>=y ) >=x ) ? ( 1 ) : ( 0 ) )
( ( TRUE>=x ) ? ( 1 ) : ( 0 ) )
```

The condition is evaluated from the inside out.

```
( ( 1>=x ) ? ( 1 ) : ( 0 ) )
```

The value of the innermost relation is TRUE. It is compared to the integer x. While this is legal in C, it is really playing footloose with the value TRUE being an integer 1, and, as in this problem, it is usually not what's wanted. (The next puzzle shows the right way to compare three values.)

```
( FALSE? ( 1 ) : ( 0 ) )
( ( 0 ) )
0
```

Operators 5.5

initially x=3, y=4, z=4

z >= y && y >= x

((z>=y)&&(y>=x))

(TRUE&&(y>=x))   Evaluating from left to right.

(TRUE&&TRUE)

(TRUE)

1

Operators 6.1

        initially x=1, y=1, z=1

        ++ x ¦¦ ++ y && ++ z

((++x)¦¦((++y)&&(++z)))	Binding operands to operators.
(2¦¦((++y)&&(++z))), and x=2	Evaluating from left to right.
(TRUE¦¦whatever)	Since the left operand of the ¦¦ is TRUE, there is no need to evaluate further. In fact, C guarantees that it will *not* evaluate further. The rule is that a logical expression is evaluated from left to right until its truth value is known. For this problem that means y and z remain 1.
TRUE, or 1	

Operators 6.2

        initially x=1, y=1, z=1

        ++ x && ++ y ¦¦ ++ z

(((++x)&&(++y))¦¦(++z))	
((TRUE&&(++y))¦¦(++z)), and x=2	
((2&&2)¦¦(++z)), and y=2	Evaluating from left to right.
(TRUE¦¦(++z))	
TRUE, or 1	z is not affected.

About evaluation order and precedence. For most operators, the order of evaluation is determined by precedence. As can be seen from the puzzles in this section, there are a few exceptions to this general rule:

- Pre- increment and decrement operators are always evaluated before their operand is considered in an expression.

- Post- increment and decrement operators are always evaluated after their operand is considered.

- Logical AND and OR are always evaluated conditionally from left to right.

Operators 6.3

```
initially x=1, y=1, z=1
++ x && ++ y && ++ z
(((++x)&&(++y))&&(++z))
((2&&2)&&(++z)), and x=2, y=2
(TRUE&&(++z))
(TRUE&&TRUE), and z=2
TRUE, or 1
```

Operators 6.4

```
initially x=-1, y=-1, z=-1
++ x && ++ y ¦¦ ++ z
(((++x)&&(++y))¦¦(++z))
((0&&(++y))¦¦(++z)), and x=0
((FALSE&&(++y))¦¦(++z))
(FALSE¦¦(++z))
```

There is no need to evaluate ++y since the left operand to && is FALSE. The value of the ¦¦ operation is still not known, however.

```
(FALSE¦¦(0)), and z=0
(FALSE¦¦FALSE)
FALSE, or 0
```

Operators 6.5

initially x = − 1 , y = − 1 , z = − 1

++ x ¦¦ ++ y && ++ z

((++x) ¦¦ ((++y) && (++z)))

(FALSE ¦¦ ((++y) && (++z))) , and x = 0

(FALSE ¦¦ (FALSE && (++z))) , and y = 0

(FALSE ¦¦ FALSE)

FALSE , or 0

Operators 6.6

initially x = − 1 , y = − 1 , z = − 1

++ x && ++ y && ++ z

(((++x) && (++y)) && (++z))

((FALSE && (++y)) && (++z)) , and x = 0

(FALSE && (++z))

FALSE , or 0

About side effects in logical expressions. As you have surely learned by now, the evaluation of a logical expression can be tricky in C because the right-hand part of the expression is evaluated *conditionally* on the value of the left-hand part. Actually, conditional evaluation is a useful property of the logical operators. The trouble arises when the right-hand part of a logical expression contains a side effect; sometimes the side effect will occur and sometimes it won't. So, while in general it is good practice to use side effects carefully, it is vital in logical expressions.

Basic Types 1.1

PRINT(d,"5")	%d format instructs printf to print the argument as a decimal number. "5" is a pointer to a character array (i.e., the address of the two character array '5', '\0').
PRINT(d,'5')	%d causes the decimal value of the character '5' to be printed.[1]
PRINT(d,5)	The integer 5 is printed in decimal.
PRINT(s,"5")	%s format instructs printf that the argument is a pointer to a character array. Since "5" is a pointer to a character array, the content of that array, 5, is printed.
PRINT(c,'5')	%c format instructs printf to translate the argument into the character its value represents. Since '5' is the encoded value for 5, 5 is printed.
PRINT(c,53)	As seen earlier, the decimal number 53 is the ASCII code value for the character 5.
PRINT(d,('5'>5))	One last time. '5' has the integer value 53 which is greater than the integer 5.

---

1. The value given here is that for the ASCII character code (see Appendix 3). The ASCII code is but one of several codes used by computers to represent characters. It will be used in this book for those few cases where it matters.

Basic Types 1.2

initially `sx=-8, ux=-8`

`PRINT(o,sx)`	%o instructs `printf` to print the argument as an octal number.
`PRINT(o,ux)`	The value -8 is a string of 1's and 0's just as valid for `unsigned` variables as for signed ones.
`PRINT(o,sx>>3)`	We have seen this problem earlier. With some versions of C, right shifting of a signed integer causes the sign bit to be copied into the vacated high order bits, thus having the desirable property of preserving sign. *Beware—this is compiler dependent!*
`PRINT(o,ux>>3)`	When right shifting an `unsigned` integer the high order bits are always filled with 0's.
`PRINT(d,sx>>3)`	In decimal, right shifting a signed -8 three places yields the expected -1 if sign is preserved, 8191 otherwise (in two's-complement on a 16-bit machine).
`PRINT(d,ux>>3)`	For an `unsigned` -8, the result is always 8191 (on a 16-bit machine).

Basic Types 2.1

`i = l = f = d = 100/3`	
`(i= (l= (f= (d= ( 100/3)) )))`	Evaluation is from right to left.
`(i= (l= (f= (d=33) )))`	Since both 100 and 3 are integers, the division is integer division and thus the quotient is truncated.
`(i= (l= (f=(double)33) )),` and `d=33`	Recall that the value of an assignment expression is the value of the right-hand side cast in the type of the left-hand side.
`(i= (l=(float)33) ),` and `f=33`	
`(i=(long)33),` and `l=33`	
`(integer)33,` and `i=33`	
`33,` an integer	

Basic Types 2.2

`d = f = l = i = 100/3`

`(d= (f= (l= (i=( 100/3)) )))`

`(d= (f= (l=(integer)33) )),` and `i=33`

`(d= (f=(long)33) ),` and `l=33`

`(d=(float)33),` and `f=33`

`((double)33),` and `d=33`

`33,` a double

Basic Types 2.3

```
i = l = f = d = 100/3.
( i= ( l= ( f= ( d= ( 100/3. )) ) ))
( i= ( l= ( f=(double)33.333333) ))
    and d=33.333333
```

3. is a **double** so the quotient retains its precision.

```
( i= ( l=(float)33.333333) )
    and f=33.33333x
```

The **printf** specification in this program is "**%.8g**", which tells **printf** to output numbers of up to eight significant digits. Seven significant digits is about the limit of precision for **floats** on the PDP-11 and VAX, so the eighth digit is unreliable. The number of significant digits is, of course, machine dependent.

```
( i=(long)33.33333x), and l=33
```

The **float** to **long** conversion is through truncation.

```
(integer)33), and i=33
33, an integer
```

Basic Types 2.4

```
d = f = l = i = (double)100/3
(d= (f= (l= (i= ((double)100) /3)))))
```

Notice that type cast has higher precedence than **/**.

```
(d= (f= (l= (i=33.333333) )))
(d= (f= (l=(integer)33.333333) ))
    and i=33
(d= (f=(long)33) ), and l=33
(d=(float)33), and f=33
((double)33), and d=33
33, a double
```

Basic Types 2.5

```
i = l = f = d = (double)(100000/3)
(i= (l= (f= (d= ((double)(100000/3)) ))))
(i= (l= (f= (d=(double)33333) )))
```
The operand to the type cast is the quotient from the integer division of 100000 by 3.

```
(i= (l= (f=(double)33333) )), and d=33333
(i= (l=(float)33333) ), and f=33333
(i=(long)33333), and l=33333
((integer)33333), and i=33333 or overflow
```
33333 cannot be represented as a 16-bit signed integer. Most implementations of C will happily permit arithmetic over- or underflow. When your calculations potentially push the limits of your machine, it is wise to insert explicit range checks.

```
33333, an integer, or overflow
```

Basic Types 2.6

```
d = f = l = i = 100000/3
(d= (f= (l= (i=100000/3) )))
(d= (f= (l=(integer)33333) ))
```
    and i=33333, or overflow

As we've seen before, 33333 is overflow for a 16-bit signed integer. For integer representations with more bits, i would get 33333, as would l, f, and d. We'll continue with the case for 16-bit integers.

```
(d= (f=(long)-32203) )
```
    and l=-32203

The result of an operation that leads to overflow is a legitimate number, just not the number expected. The 33333 is lost, regardless of future type casts.

```
(d=(float)-32203), and f=-32203
((double)-32203), and d=-32203
-32203, a double
```

About numbers. The treatment of numbers is not one of C's strong points. C does not provide a way to catch arithmetic errors even if the hardware so obliges. The range of the numerical data types is fixed by the compiler writer; there is no way to specify a range in the language. To achieve range checking, about the best one can do is explicitly test the value of variables at critical points in a calculation.

Basic Types 3.1

           initially d=3.2, i=2

           x = (y=d/i)*2

           (x=(y=3.2/2)*2)

(x=(y=1.6)*2)	3.2, a double, is of higher type than 2, an int. Thus the quotient is a double.
(x=1*2), and y=1	y, an int, gets 1.6 truncated.

           (x=2)

           2, and x=2

Basic Types 3.2

           initially d=3.2, i=2

           y = (x=d/i)*2

           (y=(x=1.6)*2)

(y=1.6*2), and x=1.6	Since x is a double, the result of the assignment is a double.
(y=3.2)	1.6, a double, determines the type of the product.
3, and y=3	y, an int, gets 3.2 truncated.

Basic Types 3.3

initially d=3.2, i=2

y = d * (x=2.5/d)

(y= d* (x=2.5/d))

(y= d*2.5/d), and x=2.5/d   x is a double, so the precision of 2.5/d is retained.

(y=2.5)

2, and y=2   y gets 2.5 truncated.

Basic Types 3.4

initially d=3.2, i=2

x = d * (y = ((int)2.9+1.1)/d)

(x= d* (y=(2+1.1)/d))   Type cast has higher precedence than +.

(x= d* (y=3.1/d))

(x= d* (y=.something))

(x=d*0), and y=0   y gets 0 regardless of the value of "something", since ".something" is between 0 and 1.

0, and x=0

About mixing types. By now you have seen enough examples of how mixing floating point and integer values in expressions can lead to surprises. It is best to avoid arithmetic with operands of mixed type. If you do need it, make the type conversions explicit by *carefully* using casts.

Control Flow 1.1

```
initially y = 1
if ( y != 0 ) x=5 ;                    The first step is to evaluate the condition.
( y != 0 )
( 1 != 0 )
TRUE
```
Since the condition is TRUE, the true part of the if statement is executed.

```
x = 5
```

Control Flow 1.2

```
initially y = 1
if ( y==0 ) x=3 ; else x=5 ;
( y==0 )                               Evaluate the condition.
FALSE
x = 5
```
Execute the false part of the if statement.

Control Flow 1.3

```
initially y = 1
x = 1
if( y<0 ) if( y>0 ) x=3;
else x=5;
```

x = 1   First x is assigned 1.

```
if( y<0 ) {
   if( y>0 ) x=3;
   else x=5;
}
```
The braces indicate statement nesting.

(y<0)

FALSE   The condition of the first if is FALSE, thus the
                                        true part is skipped. The else clause is contained
                                        in the true part of the first if since it belongs to
                                        the second if. The rule in C is that an else
                                        clause belongs to the closest if that can accept it.

Control Flow 1.4

```
initially y = 1
if( z=y<0 ) x=3;
else if( y==0 ) x=5;
else x=7;
```

(z=(y<0))   Begin by evaluating the first condition. We will
                                        use parentheses, as before, to indicate the binding
                                        of operands to operators.

(z=(1<0))

(z=FALSE)

FALSE, and z=0

(y==0)   Since the condition of the first if statement is
                                        FALSE, the false part of the if is executed. The
                                        false part is another if statement, so its condition
                                        is evaluated.

FALSE

x = 7   The condition is FALSE, thus the false part of the
                                        second if statement is executed.

Control Flow 1.5

```
initially y = 1
if( z=(y==0) ) x=5; x=3
if( z=(y==0) ) { x=5; } x=3;
```
The true part of an `if` is the single statement or block following the condition for the `if`.

```
( z=(y==0) )
```
Evaluate the condition.

```
( z=FALSE )

FALSE, and z=0

x = 3
```
Since the `if` statement does not have a false part, control falls through to the next statement.

Control Flow 1.6

```
initially y = 1
if( x=z=y ); x=3;
if( x=z=y ) { ; } x=3;
```
The true part of the `if` is a null statement.

```
( x=(z=y)) )
```
Evaluate the condition.

```
( x=(z=1))

( x=1 ), and z=1

TRUE, and x=1

x = 3
```
The `if` condition is TRUE, so the true part of the `if` is executed. The true part is a null statement and has no effect. Finally, the statement following the `if` is executed.

Control Flow 2.1

```
initially x=0 , y=0
while( y<10 ) ++y; x += y;
```

`while( y<10 ) ++y;`	Begin by analyzing the factors that control the execution of the `while` statement:
`( y<10 )`	The *loop condition*. The body of the loop is executed as long as the loop condition evaluates to TRUE.
`( y>=10 )`	The *exit condition*. The exit condition, the negation of the loop condition, is TRUE upon a normal termination of the loop.
`y = 0`	The *initial value* of the control variable. This is the value of the control variable during the first iteration of the loop body.
`++y`	The *effect* on the control variable of executing the body of the loop.
`y = 0 through 9 in the loop`	y=0 the first time in the loop. Each time through the body y is incremented by 1.
`y = 10 on exit`	When y=10 the loop condition evaluates to FALSE and the iteration terminates.
`x += y;`	Control passes to the statement following the loop body.
`x = 0+10`	
`x = 10`	

Control Flow 2.2

initially x=0 , y=0
while(y<10) x += ++y;

(y<10)	The loop condition.
(y>=10)	The exit condition.
y = 0	The initial value of the control variable.
++y	The effect of the loop on the control variable.
y = 0 through 9 in the loop	As in the previous problem.
x += ++y	x gets the sum of the values of y (after y is incremented) in the loop.
x = 55	The sum of the integers 1 to 10.
y = 10 on exit	

Control Flow 2.3

initially y=1
while(y<10) { x = y++; z = ++y; }

(y<10)	The loop condition.
(y>=10)	The exit condition.
y = 1	The initial value of the control variable.
y++ , ++y	The effect of the loop on the control variable.
y = 1,3,5,7,9 in the loop	y=1 the first time in the loop and is incremented by 2 each time through the loop.
x = 1,3,5,7,9	x takes on the value of y in the loop before it is incremented.
z = 3,5,7,9,11	z takes on the value of y in the loop after it has been incremented by 2.
y = 11 on exit	

Control Flow 2.4

`for( y=1; y<10; y++ ) x=y;`	The `for` statement aggregates the controlling factors of the loop.
`y<10`	Loop condition.
`y>=10`	Exit condition.
`y=1`	Initial value.
`y++`	Effect.
`y` = 1 through 9 in the loop	
`x` = 1 through 9	`x` gets the value of `y` in the body of the loop.
`y` = 10 on exit	

Control Flow 2.5

`for( y=1; (x=y)<10; y++ ) ;`	
`y<10`	Loop condition.
`y>=10`	Exit condition.
`y=1`	Initial value.
`y++`	Effect.
`y` = 1 through 9 in the loop	
`x` = 1 through 10	`x` gets the value of `y` just before the evaluation of the loop condition. Note that the condition is evaluated one time more than the body is executed.
`y` = 10 on exit	

Control Flow 2.6

```
for( x=0,y=1000; y>1; x++,y/=10 )
   PRINT2(d,x,y);
```

`y>1`	Loop condition.
`y<=1`	Exit condition.
`y=1000`	Initial value.
`y/=10`	Effect.
`y = 1000,100,10` in the loop	
`x = 0,1,2` in the loop	`x=0` from the `for` statement initialization. `x` is incremented after the body and *before* the test. (The `PRINT2` statement is in the body.)
`y = 1` on exit	
`x = 3` on exit	

Control Flow 3.1

```
initially i=in=high=low=0, input="PI=3.14159, approximately"
```

```
while( c=(NEXT(i)!=EOS) )
```
The loop condition effectively is `NEXT(i)!=EOS`, where `NEXT(i)` successively takes on the character values from `input`. `c` gets the truth value of `NEXT(i)!=EOS`, which, by definition, is `TRUE` in the loop and `FALSE` on exit.

```
if( 1<'0' ) low++
```
`c` is always 1 in the loop, so `low` is always incremented (1 < 060).

```
while( c=(I!=EOS) )
```
The iteration continues until all the characters in `input` have been read. C uses the ASCII `nul` character, `00`, as the end of string marker.

Control Flow 3.2

```
initially i=in=high=low=0, done=FALSE,
          input="PI=3.14159, approximately"
```

```
while( (c=NEXT(i))!=EOS && !done )
```
`c` successively takes on the value of each character from `input`.

```
if( 'P'<'0' )
```
The first time through the loop `c='P'`, hence the `if` condition is `FALSE`.

```
else if( 'P'>'9' )
```
`TRUE`, and `high++`.

```
while( 'I'!=EOS && !done )
```
Back at the loop test. (The `if` statement comparing `low`, `high`, and `in` with `ENUF` is outside the loop, indentation to the contrary.) Since `done` is not effected within the loop, the iteration ends when `c=EOS`. In the loop, the counters `low`, `in`, and `high` are incremented depending upon the value of `c` with respect to the digit characters `'0'` to `'9'`.

Control Flow 3.3

initially `i=in=high=low=0, done=FALSE,` `input="PI=3.14159, approximately"`	
`while( (c=NEXT(i))!=EOS && !done ) {`	c successively takes on the value of each character from input.
`if( 'P'<'0' )`	FALSE.
`else if( 'P'>'9' )`	TRUE.
`done = (++high==ENUF)`	high, after being incremented, is not equal to ENUF, so done is assigned FALSE. high=1.
`while( 'I'!=EOS && !done )`	TRUE.
`if( 'I'<'0' )`	FALSE.
`else if( 'I'>'9' )`	TRUE.
`done = (++high==ENUF)`	high=2, done=FALSE.
`while( '='!=EOS && !done )`	TRUE.
`if( '='<'0' )`	FALSE.
`else if( '='>'9' )`	TRUE.
`done = (++high==ENUF)`	high=3, done=TRUE.
`while( '3'!=EOS && !done )`	done=TRUE, so !done=FALSE, and the loop terminates.

Control Flow 4.1

`char input[]="SSSWILTECH1\1\11W\1WALLMP1"`	The character array `input` is initialized to the character string `"SSS...MP1"`.
`for(i=2; (c=input[2])!='\0';`	c takes character values from `input` beginning at the third character.
`switch('S') {`	The first time through the `switch` statement c=`'S'`.
`default: putchar('S')`	The `default` case is taken since none of the case labels match `'S'`. S is printed.
`continue`	The `continue` statement forces the next iteration of the innermost enclosing loop, in this case, the `for` loop. Notice that `continue` is effectively a branch to the reinitialization expression of the `for`.
`for( ; (c=input[3])!='\0'; i++) {`	c gets the fourth character from `input`.
`switch('W') {`	c=`'W'`.
`default: putchar('W'); continue`	As before, W is printed.
`...`	Similarly for i=4, c=`'I'`.
`switch('L') {`	i=5, c=`'L'`.
`case 'L': continue`	The `'L'` case is taken; nothing is printed.

In the `for` loop:

`i=5, c='L';`	Nothing is printed.
`i=6, c='T';`	T printed.
`i=7, c='E';`	Nothing is printed.
`i=8, c='C';`	C is printed.
`i=9, c='H';`	H is printed.
`switch('1') {`	i=10, c=`'1'`.

`case '1': break`	The `break` statement forces an exit from the innermost enclosing loop or `switch`. In this case, it causes a branch to the statement following the end of the `switch`.
`putchar(' ')`	A space is printed.
`for( ; (c=input[11])!='\0'; i++) {`	Back at the top of the `for` loop.
`switch('\1') {`	The character constant `'\n'`, where n is up to four octal digits, yields a character with the octal value n. For instance, `\0` yields the ASCII character `nul`, and `\101` the character A.
`case 1:`	Case labels may be either character or integer constants. `\1` matches the integer 1 since C automatically coerces `char` to `int`.
`while( (c=input[++i])!='\1' && c!='\0') ;`	The exit condition for the `while` is either `c=='\1'` or end of string. Each time the `while` test is made, `i` is incremented by 1, thus, the loop advances `i` past the characters of `input` to either the next `'\1'` character or the end of string.

In the while loop:

`i=12, c='\11';`	Nothing is printed.
`i=13, c='W';`	Nothing is printed.
`i=14, c='\1';`	The `while` loop terminates.
`case 9: putchar('S')`	The statements from each case follow one another directly; there is no implied `break` between cases. Case 9 follows case 1. S is printed.
`case 'E': case 'L': continue`	Cases `'E'` and `'L'` follow case 9.

```
for( ; (c=input[15]); i++) {
```
Again, back to the top of the
for loop.

In the for loop:

```
    i=15, c='W';
```
W is printed.

```
    i=16, c='A';
```
A is printed.

```
    i=17, c='L';
```
Nothing is printed.

```
    i=18, c='L';
```
Nothing is printed.

```
    i=19, c='M';
```
M is printed.

```
    i=20, c='P';
```
P is printed.

```
    i=21, c='1';
```
Space is printed.

```
    i=22, c='\0';
```
The for loop terminates.

```
putchar('\n')
```

Programming Style 1.1

The need for a `continue` statement can often be eliminated by altering a test condition. The resulting code is sometimes remarkably cleaner.

For this problem, simply negating the test to the `if` statement will do.

```
while(A)
        if(!B)  C;
```

Programming Style 1.2

The `do...while` is another of the C constructs that can sometimes be replaced to advantage. If either a `do...while` or a `while` can be used, the `while` is always preferred since it has the desirable property that the condition is tested before every iteration of the loop. That the condition is not tested before the first iteration of a `do...while` loop has been the source of many a program bug.

In this problem, the `if` and `do...while` are redundant; they are effecting a `while`.

```
do {                         First, eliminate the continue.
      if(A) { B; C; }
} while(A);
```

```
while(A) {                   Then replace the do...while and if with a while.
      B; C;
}
```

Programming Style 1.3

The problem of deeply nested if statements is well known to most experienced programmers: by the time one gets to the innermost condition the surrounding conditions have been forgotten or obscured. The counter approach is to qualify each condition fully, but this tends to generate long conditions that are obscure from the start. Alas, good judgement must prevail!

Here are two possibilities for this problem:

```
if( A && B && C ) D;
else if( !A && B && C ) E;
else if( !A && B && !C ) F;
```

or,

```
if( B )
      if( A && C ) D;
      else if( !A && C ) E;
      else if( !A && !C ) F;
```

Programming Style 1.4

This problem has a straightforward idea hierarchy:

- while there are more characters on the line
- multiway switch based on character type

    - return ALPHA
    - return DIGIT
    - return OTHER.

This translates easily into C:

```
while( (c=getchar()) != '\n' ) {
     if( c>='a' && c<='z' ) return(ALPHA);
     else if( c>='0' && c<='9' ) return(DIGIT);
     else if( c!=' ' && c!='\t' ) return(OTHER);
}
return(EOL);
```

Programming Style 2.1

```
done = i = 0;
while( i<MAXI && !done ) {
     if( (x/=2) > 1 ) i++;
     else done++;
}
```

The first observation is that the if...continue construct is effecting an if...else. So make it an if...else!

```
i = 0;
while( i<MAXI && (x/=2)>1 ) i++;
```

Then it becomes clear that

- one loop condition is done equal to FALSE;
- done is FALSE as long as the if condition is TRUE;
- thus, one loop condition is (x/2)>1.

Make it explicit!

```
for( i=0; i<MAXI && (x/=2)>1; i++ ) ;
```

A while statement that is preceded by an initialization and that contains a change of the loop control variable is exactly a for statement.

Programming Style 2.2

There are usually many ways to express an idea in C. A useful guideline is to group ideas into chunks. C provides a hierarchy of packaging for these chunks:

- the lowest level ideas become expressions;
- expressions are grouped together into statements;
- statements are grouped together into blocks and functions.

In this problem there is a two level idea hierarchy. At the lowest level are the expressions B, D, F, and G. They are related as the mutually exclusive cases of a multiway switch. A cohesive representation for a general multiway switch is the if...else if construction.

```
if(A) B;
else if(C) D;
else if(E) F;
else G;
return;
```

Programming Style 2.3

The key observation in this problem is that the underlying structure is a three-way switch with mutually exclusive cases.

```
plusflg = zeroflg = negflg = 0;

if( a>0 ) ++plusflg;
else if( a==0 ) ++zeroflg;
else ++negflg;
```

Programming Style 2.4

```
i = 0;
while( (c=getchar())!=EOF && c!='\n' ) {
    if( c!='\n' && c!='\t' ) {
        s[i++] = c;
        continue;
    }
    if( c=='\t' ) c = ' ';
    s[i++] = c;
}
```

Reformatting the statements to indicate nesting is a good start. Then look closer at the break and continue statements to see if they are really necessary. The break goes easily by adding the negation of the break condition to the condition for the while.

```
i = 0;
while( (c=getchar())!=EOF && c!='\n' ) {
    if( c!='\t' ) {
        s[i++] = c;
        continue;
    }
    if( c=='\t' ) s[i++] = ' ';
}
```

The first if condition can then be reduced. (c != '\n' is now a loop condition, hence it must always be TRUE in the if test.)

```
i = 0;
while( (c=getchar())!=EOF && c!='\n' )
    if( c!='\t' ) s[i++] = c;
    else s[i++] = ' ';
```

The continue statement is effecting an if...else.

```
for( i=0; (c=getchar())!=EOF && c!='\n'; i++ )
    if( c!='\t' ) s[i] = c;
    else s[i] = ' ';
```

or,

```
for( i=0; (c=getchar())!=EOF && c!='\n'; i++ )
    s[i] = c!='\t' ? c : ' ';
```

Finally, it is clear that s[i] gets the next character if the character is not a tab, otherwise it gets a space. In other words, the code merely replaces tabs by spaces. The last two versions show this quite clearly while also pointing out the close relationship of the if to the conditional. In this example, the if emphasizes the test for tab and the conditional emphasizes the assignment to s[i].

Programming Style 2.5

```
if( j>k ) y = j / (x!=0 ? x : NEARZERO);
else y = k / (x!=0 ? x : NEARZERO);
```

In this problem it is quite clear that $x!=0$ is not the primary idea; the test simply protects against division by zero. The conditional nicely subordinates the zero check.

```
y = MAX(j,k) / (x!=0 ? x : NEARZERO);
```

A case can be made that the assignment to y is the primary idea, subordinating both tests. (MAX returns the greater of its two arguments.)

Storage Classes 1.1

`int i=0;`	`i.0 = 0` (The notation x.*n* is used to reference the variable x defined at block level *n*.[1]) The storage class of `i.0` is `extern`.[2] The scope of `i.0` is potentially any program loaded with this file. The lifetime of `i.0` is the full execution time of this program.
`main( )`	
`{`	Block level is now 1.
`auto int i=1;`	`i.1 = 1` (i at level 1). The storage class of `i.1` is `auto`. The scope of `i.1` is the function `main`. The lifetime of `i.1` is the duration of the execution of `main`.
`PRINT1(d,i.1);`	When two variables have the same name, the innermost variable is referenced when the name is given; the outer variable is not directly accessible.
`{`	Block level is now 2.
`int i=2;`	`i.2 = 2`. The storage class of `i.2` is `auto`, the default storage class for variables defined in block 1 or deeper. The scope of `i.2` is block 2 and its lifetime is the duration of execution of block 2.
`PRINT1(d,i.2);`	
`{`	Block level is now 3.
`i.2+=1;`	`i.2 = 3`.
`PRINT1(d,i.2);`	`i.2` is printed since it is the innermost variable named i.
`}`	Block level returns to 2.
`PRINT1(d,i.2);`	`i.2` is printed again.
`}`	Block level returns to 1; `i.2` dies.
`PRINT1(d,i.1);`	With the death of `i.2`, `i.1` became the innermost variable named i.
`}`	Block level returns to 0.

---

1. The *block level* at any point in the text of a program is the count of left braces ({) minus the count of right braces (}). In other words, it is the number of textually open blocks. The outermost level of a program, i.e., no blocks open, is block level 0.

2. You might ask why the storage class of i is not explicitly declared here using the `extern` keyword. Unless declared otherwise, the storage class for variables defined at block level 0 is `extern`. Tagging a variable with `extern` does not define the variable. Instead, it tells the compiler that the variable has been defined elsewhere at block level 0.

Storage Classes 2.1

`int i=LOW;`	i.0 = 0.
`main( )`	
`{`	
`auto int i=HIGH;`	i.1 = 5.
`reset(i.1/2);`	The function `reset` is called with the value i.1/2, or 2. Its execution has no effect on i.1.
`PRINT1(d,i.1);`	
`reset(i.1=i.1/2);`	`reset` is again called with i.1/2. This time i.1 is assigned 2 as a side effect of the function call. Again, `reset` has no effect on i.1.
`PRINT1(d,i.1);`	
`i.1=reset(i.1/2);`	i.1 gets the value returned by `reset` called with i.1/2. We will expand the function call in line.
`    int reset(1)`	The type of the value returned by a function is specified in its declaration. `reset` returns a value of type `int`.
`    { (int i=1;)`	i.reset = 1. Parameters in a function behave like initialized local variables. We indicate these implied assignments by surrounding them with parentheses.
`    i.reset = i.reset<=2 ? 5 : 2;`	i.reset = 5.
`    return(i.reset);`	`reset` returns the integer 5; thus, i.1 = 5.
`    }`	
`PRINT1(d,i.1)`	
`workover(i.1);`	`workover` is passed the value of i.1; i.1 is not affected by the call. We'll expand `workover` since it includes a PRINT.
`    workover(5)`	If not otherwise specified, functions return an `int`.
`    { (int i=5;)`	i.workover = 5.
`    i.workover = 0 * whatever;`	i.workover = 0.
`    PRINT1(d,i.workover);`	
`    return(i.workover);`	`workover` returns 0, but the value is ignored in the calling routine.
`    }`	
`PRINT1(d,i.1);`	
`}`	

Storage Classes 3.1

```
int i=1;
main( )
{
auto int i,j;
i.1 = reset( );
  reset( )
  {
  return( i.0 );



  }
for( j.1=1; j.1<3; j.1++ ) {
PRINT2( d,i.1,j.1 );
PRINT1( d,next( i.1 ));
  int next( 1 )
  { (int j=1;)
  return( j.next=i.0++ );




  }
PRINT1( d,last( i.1 ));
  int last( 1 )
  { (int j=1;)
  static int i=10;
```

i.0 = 1.

i.1 and j.1 are defined, but not yet set.

i.1 gets the value returned by reset.

As reset has neither a parameter nor a local variable named i, the reference to i must refer to i.0. reset returns 1, so i.1 = 1.

j.1 = 1.

j.next = 1.

i.0 = 2 but next returns 1 since the increment occurs after the value of i.0 is taken.

The return statement references i.0 since next knows of no other i. j.next dies with the return.

j.last = 1.

i.last = 10.
last has a local variable named i initialized to 10. The storage class of i is static, which means that i is initialized when the program is loaded and dies when the program is terminated.

```
        return( j.last=i.last-- );
```
i.last = 9 but 10 is returned since the decrement occurs after the value is taken.

j.last dies with the return, but i.last lives on. Thus, when last is called again, i.last will be 9.

```
    }
PRINT1(d,new(i.1+j.1));
    int new(2)
    { (int i=2;)
    int j=10;
        return(i.new=j.new+=i.new);
```
i.new = 2.

j.new = 10.

j.new = 12, i.new = 12, and 12 is returned.
j.new and i.new die with the return.

```
    }
for( j.1=1; j.1<3; j.1++ ) {
```
j.1 = 2.
Back to the for statement. For this iteration we will generalize about the effect of each statement.

```
    PRINT2(d,i.1,j.1);
```
The effect of executing the loop body is to increment j.1 by one. The loop has no effect on the value of i.1.

```
    PRINT1(d,next(i.1));
```
next ignores the value it is passed and returns the current value of i.0. As a side effect of executing next, i.0 is incremented by one.

```
    PRINT1(d,last(i.1));
```
last also ignores the value of its passed argument. It returns the current value of its local static variable, i.last. As a side effect of executing last, i.last is decremented by one.

```
    PRINT1(d,new(i.1+j.1));
```
new returns the value of its argument plus 10. There are no lasting side effects.

```
    }
    }
```

Storage Classes 4.1

```int i=1;```	i.0 = 1.
```main()```	
```{```	
```auto int i,j;```	
```i.1 = reset();```	
```extern int i;```	The ```extern``` statement tells the compiler that i is an external variable defined elsewhere, possibly in another file. Here i refers to i.0.
```reset()```	
```{```	
```return(i.0);```	i.0 is the external i referenced in ```reset```. i.1 = 1.
```}```	
```for(j.1=1; j.1<3; j.1++){```	j.1 = 1.
```PRINT2(d,i.1,j.1);```	
```PRINT1(d,next(i.1));```	
```static int i=10;```	The second source file begins with an external definition of a variable named i. This definition might appear to be in conflict with the external variable i defined in the first file. The designation ```static```, however, tells the compiler that this i is known only within the current file. In other words, it is only known within the functions ```next```, ```last```, and ```new```. We will reference it by i.nln; i.nln = 10.
```next()```	
```{```	The declaration of ```next``` does not include any arguments. The value passed by ```main``` is ignored.
```return(i.nln+=1);```	i.nln = 11 and ```next``` returns 11.
```}```	
```PRINT1(d,last(i.1));```	
```last()```	
```{```	
```return(i.nln-=1);```	i.nln = 10 and ```last``` returns 10. ```last``` references the same i previously incremented by ```next```.
```}```	

```
PRINT1(d,new(i.1+j.1));
   new(2)
   { (int i=2;)                    i.new = 2.
   static int j=5;                 j.new = 5.
   return(i.new=j.new=5+2);        j.new = 7, i.new = 7, and 7 is returned.
                                   i.nln is unaffected, i.new will die with the
                                   return, and j.new will be 7 when new is called
                                   again.

   }
for( j.1=1; j.1<3; j.1++ ) {       j.1 = 2.
                                   In this iteration we will generalize about the
                                   effect of each statement.


PRINT2(d,i.1,j.1);                 The effect of the loop is to increment j.1 by
                                   one.

PRINT1(d,next(i.1));               next increments i.nln and returns the
                                   resulting value.

PRINT1(d,last(i.1));               last decrements i.nln and returns the
                                   resulting value.

PRINT1(d,new(i.1+j.1));            new adds its argument to j.new and returns
                                   the resulting sum.

   }
}
```

Pointers and Arrays 1.1

`int a[] = {0,1,2,3,4};`	a is defined to be an array of five integers, with elements `a[i]=i` for i from 0 to 4.
`for( i=0; i<=4; i++ )`	i takes on the values 0 to 4.
`PR(d,a[i]);`	`a[i]` successively accesses each element of a.

Pointers and Arrays 1.2

`int *p;`	Declarations of the form *type* `*x` tell the compiler that when `*x` appears in an expression it yields a value of type *type*. x is a pointer-to-*type* taking on values that are addresses of elements of type *type*. *Type* is the base type of x. In this problem, p is declared as a pointer-to-integer; the base type of p is `int`.
`for( p= &a[0];`	`&a[0]` evaluates to the address of `a[0]`.
`p<=&a[4];`	Array elements are stored in index order, that is, `a[0]` precedes `a[1]` precedes `a[2]` and so on. Thus p, initialized to `&a[0]`, is less than `&a[4]`.
`PR(d,*p);`	`*p` evaluates to the integer stored at the address contained in p. Since p holds `&a[0]`, `*p` is `a[0]`.
`p++ )`	When applied to a pointer variable, the increment operator advances the pointer to the next element of its base type. What actually happens is that the pointer is incremented by `sizeof(`*base type*`)` bytes. C does not test to insure that the resulting address is really that of a valid element of the base type. In this problem, p is advanced to the next element of a.
`p<=&a[4]`	p is again tested against the end of the array. The loop is terminated when p points beyond the last element of a. While in the loop, p points successively to each element of a in index order.

Pointers and Arrays 1.3

`for( p=&a[0],i=1; i<=5; i++ )`	p points to the start of the array a. i takes on the values 1 through 5.
`PR(d,p[i]);`	p[i] successively refers to the elements of a. p[5] points outside of the array.

About arrays and indices. Though by far the most common use of [ ] is to represent array subscripting, [ ] actually is a general indexing operator. x[i] is defined to be *(x+i), where x is usually an address and i is usually integral. The rules of address arithmetic apply, so i is in units of sizeof(*base type* of x). (It should by now be clear why array indices begin at 0. An array name is actually a pointer to the first element in the array. An index is the offset from the array start. The offset to the first element from the array start is 0.) In this last problem, i is used to index off p. p[i] = *(p+i) = *(a+i) = a[i]. i goes from 1 to 5. When i=5, p+i points just beyond the end of the array, hence the value at p+i is unknown. This is such a common mistake, it is worth noting again: *an array with n elements has indices of 0 through n-1.*

Pointers and Arrays 1.4

`for( p=a,i=0;`	p gets the address of the first element of a.
`p+i <= a+4;`	p=a, i=0, so p+i=a+0, which is less than a+4.
`PR(d,*(p+i));`	*(p+i) = *(a+0) = a[0].
`p++, i++ )`	p points to the second element of a, i is 1.
`p+i <= a+4`	p=a+1, i=1, thus p+i=a+2.
`PR(d,*(p+i));`	*(p+i) = a[2].
`p++, i++`	p=a+2, i=2.
`p+i <= a+4`	p+i = a+4.
`PR(d,*(p+i));`	*(p+i) = a[4].
`p++, i++`	p=a+3, i=3.
`p+i <= a+4`	p+i = a+6, and the loop terminates.

Pointers and Arrays 1.5

```
for( p=a+4;
```
p points to the fifth element of a.

```
p >= a;
```
The loop terminates when p points below a.

```
PR(d,*p);
```
The integer pointed to by p is printed.

```
p--
```
p is decremented to the preceding element.

Pointers and Arrays 1.6

```
for( p=a+4,i=0; i<=4; i++ )
```
p points to the last element of a, i goes from 0 to 4.

```
PR(d,p[-i]);
```
The element -i away from the last element of a is printed.

Pointers and Arrays 1.7

```
for( p=a+4; p>=a; p-- )
```
p points successively to the elements of a from the last to the first.

```
PR(d,a[p-a]);
```
p-a evaluates to the offset from the start of the array to the element pointed to by p. In other words, p-a is the index of the element pointed to by p.

Pointers and Arrays 2.1

`int a[] = {0,1,2,3,4}`	a is initialized to be an array of five integers.
`int *p[] = {a,a+1,a+2,a+3,a+4};`	When encountered in an expression, `*p[ ]` evaluates to an integer, thus `p[ ]` must point to an integer, and `p` is an array of pointer-to-integer. The five elements of `p` initially point to the five elements of `a`.
`int **pp = p;`	`**pp` evaluates to an integer, hence `*pp` must point to an integer, and `pp` must point to a pointer-to-integer. `pp` initially points to `p[0]`.

Figure 2.1 illustrates the relationships between pp, p, and a.

Figure 2.1

Pointers and Arrays 2.2

`PRINT2(d,a,*a);`

As noted earlier, the name of an array is synonymous with the address of the first element in the array. The value of a is thus the address of the array a, and *a is equivalent to a[0].

`PRINT3(d,p,*p,**p);`

p evaluates to the address of the first element of the array p, *p yields the value of the first element, i.e., p[0], and **p yields the integer at the address contained in p[0], i.e., the value at a[0].

`PRINT3(d,pp,*pp,**pp);`

pp yields the contents of pp, which is the address of p. *pp yields the value at p, or p[0]. And **pp yields the integer pointed to by p[0], or a[0].

Pointers and Arrays 2.3

`pp++`

pp is a pointer to pointer-to-integer (the base type of pp is pointer-to-integer), so pp++ increments pp to point to the next pointer in memory. The effect of pp++ is indicated by the bold arrow in Figure 2.3-1.

`pp-p`

pp points to the second element of the array p, p[1]. The value of pp is thus p+1.
pp-p = (p+1)-p, which is 1.

`*pp-a`

pp points to p[1] and *pp points to the second element of the array a. The value of *pp is thus a+1. *pp-a = (a+1)-a.

`**pp`

*pp points to a[1], so **pp yields the contents at a[1].

`*pp++`

*(pp++)
Unary operators group from right to left. First the increment is bound, then the indirection. The bold arrow in Figure 2.3-2 shows the effect of the increment.

`*++pp`

*(++pp)
(Figure 2.3-3)

`++*pp`

++(*pp)
(Figure 2.3-4)

Figure 2.3-1

Figure 2.3-2

Figure 2.3-3

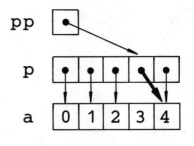

Figure 2.3-4

Pointers and Arrays 2.4

Figure 2.4-1 pp=p

Figure 2.4-2 *(*(pp++))

Figure 2.4-3 *(++(*pp))

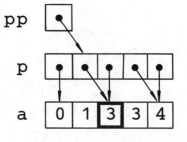

Figure 2.4-4 ++(*(*pp))

Pointers and Arrays 3.1

```
int a[3][3] = {
    { 1,2,3 },
    { 4,5,6 },
    { 7,8,9 }
};
```

a is a 3 by 3 matrix with rows 123, 456, and 789. a[i][j] evaluates to an integer at offset j from the start of row i. a[i] yields the address of the first element of row i. And a yields the address of the first row of the matrix a. Thus a is a pointer to three-element-integer-array, and a[ ] is a pointer-to-integer.

```
int *pa[3] = {
    a[0],a[1],a[2]
};
```

*pa[ ] evaluates to an integer, thus pa[ ] is a pointer-to-integer and pa is an array of pointer-to-integer. pa[0] is initialized to the first element of the first row of a, pa[1] to the first element in the second row, and pa[2] to the first element in the third row.

```
int *p = a[0];
```

p is a pointer-to-integer initially pointing to the first element of the first row of the matrix a.

Figure 3.1 illustrates the relationships between a, pa, and p.

Figure 3.1

Pointers and Arrays 3.2

`for(i=0; i<3; i++)`	i goes from 0 to 2 in the loop.
`a[i][2-i]`	`a[i][2-i]` selects the diagonal from `a[0][2]` to `a[2][0]`.
`*a[i]`	`a[i]` yields the address of the first element of the ith row in the matrix `a`. `*a[i]` yields the value of the first element of the ith row.
`*(*(a+i)+i)`	`a+i` yields the address of the ith row of `a`. `*(a+i)` yields the address of the first element from the ith row. `*(a+i)+i` yields the address of the ith element from the ith row. And `*(*(a+i)+i)` gets the integer value from the ith element of the ith row.

Pointers and Arrays 3.3

`for(i=0; i<3; i++)`	i goes from 0 to 2 in the loop.
`pa[i]`	`pa[i]` accesses the ith element of `pa`. `*pa[i]` accesses the integer pointed to by the ith element of `pa`.
`p[i]`	`p` points to the first element of the first row in the matrix `a`. Since the base type of `p` is int, `p[i]` yields the ith element of the first row in `a`.

About array addresses. We have noted several times that the address of an array and the address of the first element in the array have the same value. In this past puzzle, we saw that `a` and `a[0]` evaluated to the same address. One difference between the address of an array and the address of the first element in the array is the *type* of the address and, hence, the unit of arithmetic on an expression containing the address. Thus, since the type of `a` is pointer to three-element-integer-array, the base type of `a` is three-element-integer-array and `a+1` refers to the next three-element-integer-array in memory. Since the type of `a[0]` is pointer-to-integer, the base type of `a[0]` is integer and `a[0]+1` refers to the next integer in memory.

Pointers and Arrays 4.1

```
char *c[] = {
    "ENTER",
    "NEW",
    "POINT",
    "FIRST"
};
```

*c[ ] evaluates to a character, so c[ ] points to characters and c is an array of pointer-to-character. The elements of c have been initialized to point to the character arrays "ENTER", "NEW", "POINT", and "FIRST".

```
char **cp[] = {
    c+3,c+2,c+1,c
};
```

**cp[ ] evaluates to a character, *cp[ ] is a pointer-to-character, and cp[ ] is a pointer-to-pointer-to-character. Thus cp is an array of pointers to pointer-to-character. The elements of cp have been initialized to point to the elements of c.

```
char ***cpp = cp;
```

***cpp evaluates to a character, **cpp points to a character, *cpp points to a pointer-to-character, and cpp points to a pointer-to-pointer-to-character.

Figure 4.1 illustrates the relationships between cpp, cp, and c.

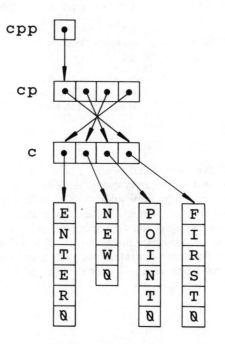

Figure 4.1

Pointers and Arrays 4.2

`*(*(++cpp))`	Increment `cpp` then follow the pointers. (Figure 4.2-1)
`(*(--(*(++cpp)))))+3`	Increment `cpp`, follow the pointer to `cp[2]`, decrement `cp[2]`, follow the pointer to `c[0]`, index 3 from the address in `c[0]`. (Figure 4.2-2)
`(*(cpp[(-2)]))+3`	Indirectly reference -2 from `cpp` yielding `cp[0]`, follow the pointer to `c[3]`, index 3 from the address in `c[3]`. (Figure 4.2-3)
`((cpp[-1])[-1])+1`	Indirectly reference -1 from `cpp` yielding `cp[1]`, indirectly reference -1 from `cp[1]` yielding `c[1]`, index 1 from the address in `c[1]`. (Figure 4.2-4)

About pointers. If you can work this puzzle correctly then you know everything you will ever need to about the mechanics of using pointers. The power of pointers lies in their generality: we can chain them together to form an endless variety of complex data structures. The danger of pointers lies in their power: complex pointer chains are seldom readable and even more seldom reliable.

Pointers and Arrays 2.4

Figure 4.2-1

Figure 4.2-2

Figure 4.2-3

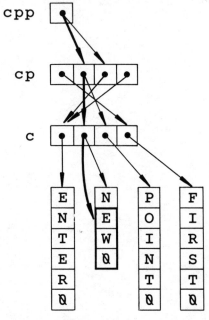

Figure 4.2-4

Structures 1.1

```
static struct S1 {
    char c[4], *s;
} s1 = { "abc", "def" };
```

The structure tag S1 refers to a structure containing a character array, c, of length 4, and a character pointer, s. The structure variable s1 is an instance of the structure S1 initialized to

```
        char  c[4]="abc",
                  *s="def"
```

The structure has been defined as static so that it may be initialized in the definition.

```
static struct S2 {
    char *cp;
    struct S1 ss1;
} s2 = { "ghi", { "jkl", "mno" } };
```

The structure tag S2 refers to a structure containing a character pointer, cp, and an instance of the structure S1, ss1. The structure variable s2 is an instance of the structure S2 initialized to

```
        char *cp="ghi";
        struct S1 ss1=
            {"jkl", "mno"};
```

Figure 1.1 depicts the structures s1 and s2.

Figure 1.1

Structures 1.2

PRINT2(c,	A character is to be printed.
(s1.c)[0]	Reference the first character of the c field of the structure s1. (Figure 1.2-1)
*(s1.s)	Reference the character pointed to by the s field of the structure s1. (Figure 1.2-2)

Figure 1.2-1

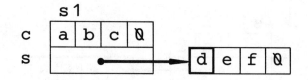

Figure 1.2-2

Structures 1.3

PRINT2(s,	A string is printed.
s1.c	Reference the string pointed to by the c field of the structure s1. Recall that c = &c[0]. (Figure 1.3-1)
s1.s	Reference the string pointed to by the s field of the structure s1. (Figure 1.3-2)

Figure 1.3-1

Figure 1.3-2

Structures 1.4

Figure 1.4-1 `s2.cp`

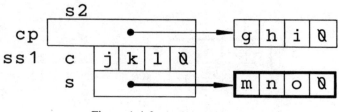

Figure 1.4-2 `(s2.ss1).s`

Structures 1.5

Figure 1.5-1 `++(s2.cp)`

Figure 1.5-2 `++((s2.ss1).s)`

Structures 2.1

```
struct S1 {
   char *s;
   int i;
   struct S1 *s1p;
};
```

S1 is declared to be a tag referring to a structure containing a character pointer, s, an integer, i, and a pointer to structure of type S1, s1p. This is only a declaration; an instance of S1 is not created.

```
static struct S1 a[] = {
   { "abcd", 1, a+1 },
   { "efgh", 2, a+2 },
   { "ijkl", 3, a }
};
```

a is a three-element array with elements of type structure S1. a has been defined as static so that it can be initialized in the definition.

```
struct S1 *p=a;
```

p is a pointer to structures of type S1. p is initialized to point to the first element of a.

Figure 2.1 depicts the array a and the pointer p.

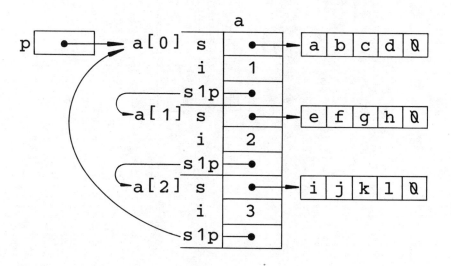

Figure 2.1

Structures 2.2

PRINT3(s,	Strings are to be printed.
(a[0]).s	Reference the string pointed to by the s field of the structure that is the first element of a. (Figure 2.2-1)
p->s	Reference the string pointed to by the s field of the structure pointed to by p. (Figure 2.2-2)
(((a[2]).s1p)->)s	Reference the string pointed to by the s field of the structure pointed to by the s1p field of the structure that is the third element of a. (Figure 2.2-3)

Figure 2.2-1

Figure 2.2-2

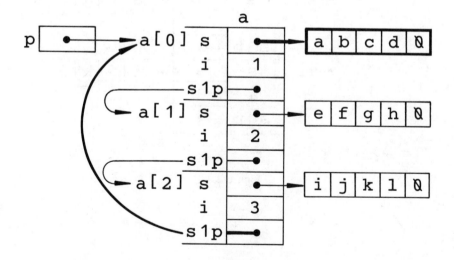

Figure 2.2-3

Structures 2.3

```
for( i=0; i<2; i++ ) {          i takes on the values of 0 and 1.

PR(d,                           Print an integer.

--((a[i]).i)                    Decrement then reference the integer in the i
                                field of the structure that is the ith element of
                                a.  (Figure 2.3-1 shows the case for i = 0)

PR(c,                           Print a character.

++(((a[i]).s)[3])               Increment then reference the fourth character
                                of the string pointed to by the s field of the
                                structure that is the ith element of a.  (Figure
                                2.3-2 shows the case for i = 0)
```

Figure 2.3-1

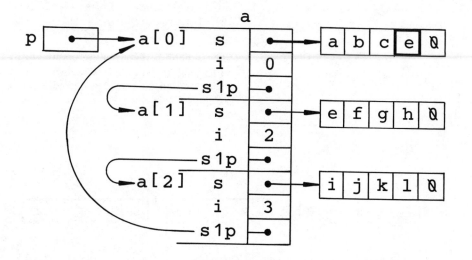

Figure 2.3-2

Structures 2.4

++(p->s)

Increment the s field of the structure pointed to by p, then output the string pointed to by the s field. (Figure 2.4-1)

a[((++p)->i)].s

First p is incremented, then the s field of the p->ith structure of a is accessed. (Figure 2.4-2)

a[--((p->s1p)->i)].s

The i field of the structure pointed to by the s1p field of the structure pointed to by p is decremented then used as an index into a. (Figure 2.4-3)

Figure 2.4-1

Figure 2.4-2

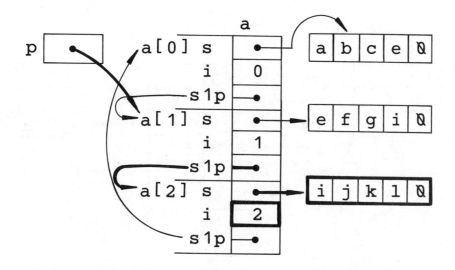

Figure 2.4-3

Structures 3.1

```
struct S1 {
   char *s;
   struct S1 *s1p;
};
```
S1 is declared to be a tag referring to a structure containing a character pointer, s, and a pointer to structure of type S1, s1p.

```
static struct S1 a[] = {
   { "abcd", a+1 },
   { "efgh", a+2 },
   { "ijkl", a }
};
```
a is a three-element array with elements of type structure S1. a has been defined as static so that it can be initialized in the definition.

```
struct S1 *(p[3]);
```
When encountered in a program statement, the expression *(p[ ]) yields a structure S1. Thus, p[ ] points to a structure S1, and p is a three-element array of pointers to structures of type S1.

Figure 3.1 depicts the arrays a and p.

Figure 3.1

Structures 3.2

```
for( i=0; i<3; i++ )
```
i takes on the values 0, 1, 2.

```
p[i] = (a[i]).s1p;
```
The ith element of p gets a copy of the pointer in the s1p field of the ith element of a. (Figure 3.2-1)

```
(p[0])->s, (*p)->s, (**p).s
```
These are all ways of saying the same thing. (Figure 3.2-2)

Figure 3.2-1

Figure 3.2-2

Structures 3.3

```
swap(*p,a);
```
p points to p[0], so *p yields the content of p[0] or &a[1]. a yields &a[0].

```
temp = (&a[1])->s;
```
Equivalently, temp = a[1].s.

```
(&a[1])->s = (&a[0])->s
```
Or, a[1].s = a[0].s

```
(&a[0])->s = temp
```
swap swaps the strings pointed to by the s fields of its arguments. (Figure 3.3-1)

```
(p[0])->s, (*p)->s
```
(Figure 3.3-2)

```
((*p)->s1p)->s
```
(Figure 3.3-3)

Figure 3.3-1

Figure 3.3-2

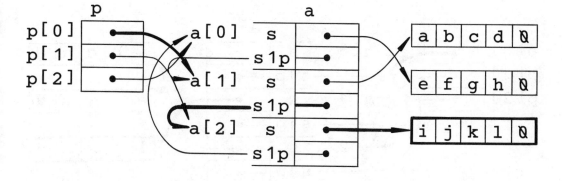

Figure 3.3-3

Structures 3.4

```
swap(p[0], (p[0])->s1p);
```
p[0] contains &a[1], (p[0])->s1p contains &a[2]. (Figure 3.4-1)

Figure 3.4-1

Figure 3.4-2 (p[0])->s

Figure 3.4-3 `(*(++(p[0]))).s`

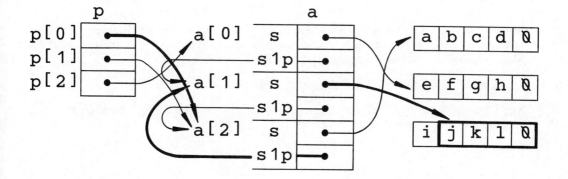

Figure 3.4-4 `++((*(++((*p)->s1p))).s)`

Preprocessor 1.1

```
int x=2;
PRINT( x*FUDGE(2) );
```
To understand the effect of a preprocessor macro, expand it in place.

```
PR(a); putchar('\n')
```
Always expand the leftmost macro. First, substitute the macro replacement string for the macro call.

```
PR( x*FUDGE(2) ); putchar('\n')
```
Then substitute the argument(s) in the call for those in the replacement string.

```
printf("a= %d\t",(int)(a))
```
Expand the leftmost macro, PR this time.

```
printf(" x*FUDGE(2) = %d\t",
    (int)(x*FUDGE(2)))
```
Substitute the macro arguments.

```
printf(" x*FUDGE(2) = %d\t",
    (int)(x*k+3.1459))
```
A macro name that occurs between quotes is not expanded. However, macro arguments are expanded wherever they occur in the macro body. Thus, x*FUDGE(2) replaces a in the macro PR, but FUDGE(2) is left unexpanded in the format of the call to printf.

```
(int)(x*2+3.14159)
```
Replace the formal parameter k by the actual parameter. Surprise! First multiply, then add (then truncate).

Beware! Macros can be a source of subtle trickery. Expanding a macro is strictly a matter of replacing one string by another. The macro preprocessor knows next to nothing about C. Most surprises can be avoided by adhering to a few conventions.

Convention 1: *Parenthesize all macro bodies that contain operators.*

The unwanted interaction between the replacement string and its context in this problem is avoided if FUDGE(k) is defined to be (k+3.14159).

Preprocessor 1.2

```
for(cel=0; cel<=100; cel+=50)
      PRINT2( cel,9./5*cel+32 );
```

```
for(cel=0; cel<=100; cel+=50)                    First expand the call to PRINT2.
      PR( cel);
PRINT( 9./5*cel+32 );
```

```
for(cel=0; cel<=100; cel+=50)                    Then expand the call to PR.
      printf(" cel= %d\t",(int)(cel));
PRINT( 9./5*cel+32 );
```

```
for(cel=0; cel<=100; cel+=50)                    Expand the call to PRINT.
      printf(" cel= %d\t",(int)(cel));
PR( 9./5*cel+32 ); putchar('\n');
```

```
for(cel=0; cel<=100; cel+=50)                    Expand the call to PR.
      printf(" cel= %d\t",(int)(cel));
printf(" 9./5*cel+32 =%d\t",
      (int)(9./5*cel+32));
putchar('\n');
```

The call to PRINT2 may look like a single statement, but it expands to three. Only the first
PR is contained within the for loop. The second PR is executed following the loop, with
cel=150.

Convention 2: *Keep macro bodies cohesive; prefer an expression to a statement, a single
statement to multiple statements.*

For this problem, using commas in place of the semicolons in the body of the PRINT
macros satisfies Convention 2.

Preprocessor 1.3

```
int x=1, y=2;
PRINT3( MAX(x++,y),x,y );
(a<b ? b : a),x,y
```
The `PRINT3` macro is, of course, expanded before `MAX`. However, to avoid obscuring the point of the puzzles, in this and following solutions the `PRINT` macros will not be expanded. The first step then is to substitute the replacement string for the call to `MAX`.

```
(x++<y ? y : x++),x,y
```
Next, substitute the actual arguments for the formal arguments.

```
(1<2 ? y : x++), and x=2
(y)
2
```
Finally, evaluate.

```
PRINT3( MAX(x++,y),x,y );
(x++<y ? y : x++),x,y
(2<2 ? y : x++), and x=3
(x++)
3, and x=4
```
Now execute the second call to `PRINT3`.

`x++` appears only once in the macro call but twice in the expansion, causing `x` to be incremented sometimes by one and sometimes by two. The burden of protecting against such unfortunate side effects can be placed either with the macro writer or the macro user.

Convention 3: *Avoid macro bodies that can cause obscure or inconsistent side effects.*
Convention 3A: *Avoid expressions with side effects in macro calls.*

In general, the problem of side effects in macros is quite tricky. Following Convention 3 often means copying arguments into local variables within the macro; this extra overhead reduces the speed advantage of macro calls over function calls. Following Convention 3A requires knowing when a routine has been coded as a macro rather than a function; at best, this violates the notion of the routine as an abstraction, and at worst, the routine may be rewritten causing the assumption no longer to be valid.

For this problem following Convention 3A preserves `MAX` intact.

Preprocessor 2.1

```
int x=1;
PRINT( -NEG(x) );
```

--a   First substitute the macro replacement string
                              for the macro call. (As before, the PRINT
                              macro will not be expanded.)

--x, and x=0   Then substitute the argument in the call for the
                              one in the replacement string.

The macro replacement string is exactly those characters that follow the closing parenthesis of the argument list. The trick in this puzzle is that the -a immediately follows the parenthesis. Still, following Convention 1 by defining NEG(a) to be (-a) produces the expected expansion. It is also a good practice to begin each replacement string with either a tab or a space.

Preprocessor 2.2

```
PRINT( weeks(10080) )
(days(10080)/7)
```
                              Replace each macro call with the macro body.
                              Notice that there is not a conflict between the
                              macro parameter mins and the macro mins.

```
((hours(10080)/24)/7)
(((10080/60)/24)/7)
1
```
                              Evaluate.

```
PRINT( days(mins(86400)) )
(hours(mins(86400))/24)
```
                              Expand the leftmost macro.

```
((mins(86400)/60)/24)
(((86400/60)/60)/24)
1
```
                              Evaluate.

Preprocessor 2.3

```
static char input = "\twhich\if?";

if(c<' ') TAB(c,i,oldi,temp);
else putchar(c);


if(c<' ')
    if(c=='\t')
        for(temp=8-(i-oldi-1)%8,oldi=i; temp; temp--)
            putchar(' ');
    else putchar(c);
```

`TAB` includes an open `if` statement. On expansion, the `if` consumes the following `else`.

Convention 4: *Make macro replacement strings complete C entities, be they expressions, statements (minus the closing semicolon), or blocks.*

For this problem, appending a null `else` clause to the `TAB` macro alleviates the difficulty. (Notice that enclosing the macro replacement string in braces, i.e., making it a block, does not solve the problem.)

About macros and functions. Very often a routine can be implemented using either a macro or a function. The advantage of using a macro is that it will be executed faster since the runtime overhead of a function call is avoided. The advantages of using a function are that none of the tricky situations we've seen in the puzzles with macros will occur, and if the routine is called several times, the implementation will probably require less memory. This leads us to the final convention for using macros:

Convention 5: *Keep macros simple. If you can't keep a macro simple, make it a function.*

APPENDICES

APPENDIX 1: Precedence Table

OPERATOR	ASSOCIATIVITY
primary: ( ) [ ] -> .	left to right
unary: ! ~ ++ -- - (*type*) * & sizeof	right to left
multiplicative: * / %	left to right
additive: + -	left to right
shift: << >>	left to right
relational: < <= > >=	left to right
equality: == !=	left to right
bitwise: &	left to right
bitwise: ^	left to right
bitwise: !	left to right
logical: &&	left to right
logical: !!	left to right
conditional: ? :	right to left
assignment: = += -= etc.	right to left
comma: ,	left to right

The precedence table illustrates the relative precedence of operators. Precedence determines the order in which operands are bound to operators. Operators receive their operands in order of decreasing operator precedence.

To determine the relative precedence of two operators in an expression find the operators in the OPERATOR column of the table. The operator higher in the list has the higher precedence. If the two operators are on the same line in the list, then look at the corresponding ASSOCIATIVITY entry. If it indicates "left to right", then the operator to the left in the expression has the higher precedence; if it indicates "right to left", then vice versa.

APPENDIX 2: Operator Summary Table

Arithmetic operators (operands are numbers and pointers)

- Additive

operator	yields	restrictions
x+y	sum of x and y	if either operand is a pointer the other must be integral†
x-y	difference of x less y	if either operand is a pointer the other must be integral or a pointer of the same base type

- Multiplicative

operator	yields	restrictions
x*y	product of x and y	x, y must not be pointer
x/y	quotient of x divided by y	x, y must not be pointer
x%y	remainder of dividing x by y	x, y must not be double, float, or pointer
-x	arithmetic negation of x	x, y must not be pointer

- Incremental

operator	yields	restrictions
x++ (x--)	x x is incremented (decremented) after use	x must be a reference to a numeric value or a pointer
++x (--x)	x+1 (x-1) x is incremented (decremented) before use	x must be a reference to a numeric value or a pointer

---

† Integral stands for the types int, char, short, long, and unsigned.

Assignment operators

operator	yields	restrictions
x=y	y cast in the type of x, x gets the value of y	x, y may be any type but array
x *op*= y	x *op* (y) cast in the type of x, x gets the value of x *op* (y)	x, y may be any type but array or structure

Bitwise operators (operands are integral)

- Logical

operator	yields	restrictions
x&y	bit by bit AND of x and y; AND yields a 1 for each place both x and y have a 1, 0 otherwise	
x¦y	bit by bit inclusive OR of x and y; inclusive OR yields a 0 for each place both x and y have a 0, 1 otherwise	
x^y	bit by bit exclusive OR of x and y; exclusive OR yields a 0 for each place x and y have the same value, 1 otherwise	
~x	one's-complement of x; 1s become 0s and 0s 1s	

- Shift

operator	yields	restrictions
x<<y	x left shifted y places, the lowest y bits get 0s	y must be positive and less than the number of bits per computer word
x>>y	x right shifted y places; the highest y bits get 0s for positive x, 1s or 0s depending on the compiler for negative x	y must be positive and less than the number of bits per computer word

Logical operators (operands are numbers and pointers)

operator	yields	restrictions
x&&y	AND of x and y: 1 if both x and y are nonzero, 0 otherwise	result is of type int
x‖y	inclusive OR of x and y: 0 if both x and y are zero, 1 otherwise	result is of type int
!x	logical negation of x: 0 if x is nonzero, 1 otherwise	result is of type int

Comparison (operands are numbers and pointers)

- Relational

operator	yields	restrictions
x<y (x>y)	1 if x is less than (greater than) y, 0 otherwise	result is of type int
x<=y (x>=y)	1 if x is less than or equal to (greater than or equal to) y, 0 otherwise	result is of type int

- Equality

operator	yields	restrictions
x==y (x!=y)	1 if x is equal to (not equal to) y, 0 otherwise	result is of type int

- Conditional

operator	yields	restrictions
x?y:z	y if x is nonzero, z otherwise	

Address operators

operator	yields	restrictions
*x	the value at the address contained in x cast in the base type of x	x must be a pointer
&x	the address of x	x must be a reference to a value
x[y]	the value at the address x+y cast in the base type of the address operand	one of the operands must be an address and the other must be integral
x.y	the value of the y field of the structure x	x must be a structure, y a structure field
x->y	the value of the y field of the structure at the address x	x must be pointer to a structure, y a structure field

Type operators

operator	yields	restrictions
(*type*)x	x cast in the type *type*	x may be any expression
sizeof x	the size in bytes of x	x may be any expression
sizeof(*type*)	the size in bytes of an object of type *type*	

Sequence operator

operator	yields	restrictions
x,y	y x is evaluated before y	x, y may be any expression

APPENDIX 3: ASCII Table

In octal

```
|000 nul|001 soh|002 stx|003 etx|004 eot|005 enq|006 ack|007 bel|
|010 bs |011 ht |012 nl |013 vt |014 np |015 cr |016 so |017 si |
|020 dle|021 dc1|022 dc2|023 dc3|024 dc4|025 nak|026 syn|027 etb|
|030 can|031 em |032 sub|033 esc|034 fs |035 gs |036 rs |037 us |
|040 sp |041  ! |042  " |043  # |044  $ |045  % |046  & |047  ' |
|050  ( |051  ) |052  * |053  + |054  , |055  - |056  . |057  / |
|060  0 |061  1 |062  2 |063  3 |064  4 |065  5 |066  6 |067  7 |
|070  8 |071  9 |072  : |073  ; |074  < |075  = |076  > |077  ? |
|100  @ |101  A |102  B |103  C |104  D |105  E |106  F |107  G |
|110  H |111  I |112  J |113  K |114  L |115  M |116  N |117  O |
|120  P |121  Q |122  R |123  S |124  T |125  U |126  V |127  W |
|130  X |131  Y |132  Z |133  [ |134  \ |135  ] |136  ^ |137  _ |
|140  ` |141  a |142  b |143  c |144  d |145  e |146  f |147  g |
|150  h |151  i |152  j |153  k |154  l |155  m |156  n |157  o |
|160  p |161  q |162  r |163  s |164  t |165  u |166  v |167  w |
|170  x |171  y |172  z |173  { |174  ¦ |175  } |176  ~ |177 del|
```

In hexadecimal

```
| 00 nul| 01 soh| 02 stx| 03 etx| 04 eot| 05 enq| 06 ack| 07 bel|
| 08 bs | 09 ht | 0a nl | 0b vt | 0c np | 0d cr | 0e so | 0f si |
| 10 dle| 11 dc1| 12 dc2| 13 dc3| 14 dc4| 15 nak| 16 syn| 17 etb|
| 18 can| 19 em | 1a sub| 1b esc| 1c fs | 1d gs | 1e rs | 1f us |
| 20 sp | 21  ! | 22  " | 23  # | 24  $ | 25  % | 26  & | 27  ' |
| 28  ( | 29  ) | 2a  * | 2b  + | 2c  , | 2d  - | 2e  . | 2f  / |
| 30  0 | 31  1 | 32  2 | 33  3 | 34  4 | 35  5 | 36  6 | 37  7 |
| 38  8 | 39  9 | 3a  : | 3b  ; | 3c  < | 3d  = | 3e  > | 3f  ? |
| 40  @ | 41  A | 42  B | 43  C | 44  D | 45  E | 46  F | 47  G |
| 48  H | 49  I | 4a  J | 4b  K | 4c  L | 4d  M | 4e  N | 4f  O |
| 50  P | 51  Q | 52  R | 53  S | 54  T | 55  U | 56  V | 57  W |
| 58  X | 59  Y | 5a  Z | 5b  [ | 5c  \ | 5d  ] | 5e  ^ | 5f  _ |
| 60  ` | 61  a | 62  b | 63  c | 64  d | 65  e | 66  f | 67  g |
| 68  h | 69  i | 6a  j | 6b  k | 6c  l | 6d  m | 6e  n | 6f  o |
| 70  p | 71  q | 72  r | 73  s | 74  t | 75  u | 76  v | 77  w |
| 78  x | 79  y | 7a  z | 7b  { | 7c  ¦ | 7d  } | 7e  ~ | 7f del|
```

ASCII (American Standard Code for Information Interchange) maps a set of control and printable characters into a set of seven bit binary numbers. The tables above show the correspondence between each character and its value. Generally, the characters below 040 octal (20 hexadecimal) are considered control characters and are not printable, though newline, tab, formfeed, etc. are located here. 040 and above are the familiar printing characters. Digits and letters are ordered in their natural way; 1 is before 2 and A is before B.

APPENDIX 4: Type Hierarchy Chart

```
double  ←  float
  ↑
long
  ↑
unsigned
  ↑
int  ←  char, short
```

The type hierarchy chart illustrates the ordering of the arithmetic types. The execution of each arithmetic operator in an expression yields a result with the type of its highest typed operand. Similarly, when two quantities are compared by a relational operator, the lower typed operand is cast in the type of the higher typed operand. The vertical arrows in the chart show the basic ordering: double is the highest type, int the lowest. The horizontal arrows indicate the automatic type conversions. That is, operands of type float are always converted to type double before being considered in an expression. Likewise, operands of types char and short are always converted to type int.